The CIVIL WAR HISTORY Series

THE BATTLE OF THE
IRONCLADS

Lieutenant Walter Raleigh Butt had been a midshipman in the U.S. Navy before the war. He resigned his commission to join the Confederacy and then was captured. Butt was imprisoned aboard the U.S.S. *Congress* until he was transferred to Fort Warren in Boston Harbor. He was exchanged in time to serve aboard the C.S.S. *Virginia* and fought at the Battle of Drewry's Bluff on May 15, 1862.

On the Cover: This is a photograph of the officers aboard the U.S.S. *Monitor* on the James River, July 1862. They are, from left to right, as follows: (bottom row) Robinson W. Hands, 3rd assistant engineer; and E.V. Gager, acting master; (middle row) Louis N. Stodder, acting master; George Frederickson, master's mate; William Flye, acting volunteer lieutenant; Daniel C. Logue, acting assistant surgeon; and Samuel Dana Green, lieutenant, executive officer; (top row) Albert B. Campbell, 2nd assistant engineer; Mark Trueman Sunstrom, 3rd assistant engineer; William F. Keeler, acting assistant paymaster; and L. Howard Newman, lieutenant, executive officer of the U.S.S. *Galena*.

THE CIVIL WAR HISTORY SERIES

THE BATTLE OF THE
IRONCLADS

JOHN V. QUARSTEIN

Sarah Goldberger, J. Michael Moore, and Tim Smith
Photo Editors

TEMPUS

Published by Arcadia Publishing,
an imprint of Tempus Publishing, Inc.
2 Cumberland Street
Charleston, SC 29401

Printed in Great Britain.

Library of Congress Catalog Card Number: Applied for.

For all general information contact Arcadia Publishing at:
Telephone 843-853-2070
Fax 843-853-0044
E-Mail arcadia@charleston.net

For customer service and orders:
Toll-Free 1-888-313-BOOK

Visit us on the internet at http://www.arcadiaimages.com

Kurtz & Allison is one of the many post-war lithographic firms to produce an inaccurate view of the March 8 and 9, 1862 engagements in Hampton Roads. This chromolithograph combines the events of both days into one dramatic scene. The *Cumberland* burns and sinks as the two ironclads duel in the distance. The shore batteries, presumably Camp Butler, are shelling the Confederate ironclad and gunboats. Brigadier General Joseph King Fenno Mansfield is in the foreground directing the action. Despite several errors, the print is a vivid scene that captures the true meaning of the events in the Hampton Roads—the power of iron over wood.

CONTENTS

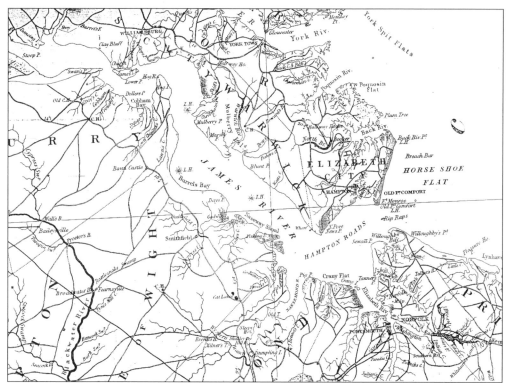

Hampton Roads, where the confluence of the James, Nansemond, and Elizabeth Rivers empties into the Chesapeake Bay, is the world's largest natural harbor. As this April 1859 version of Herman Boyle's 1825 map indicates, Hampton Roads provided a virtual amphitheater for the Confederates and Federals stationed along its shores to observe the dramatic events of March 8 and 9, 1862.

This scene, created by noted Civil War artist J.O. Davidson, depicts the dramatic ramming of the U.S.S. *Cumberland* by the C.S.S. *Virginia* on March 8, 1862.

INTRODUCTION

When the Confederate batteries encircling Charleston Harbor opened fire on Fort Sumter during the early morning of April 12, 1861, the bombardment set in motion a naval race, which resulted in the first battle between ironclad ships. Little did the Confederates realize that soon their harbors would be blockaded by the Union fleet attempting to sever the vital link between the agrarian South and industrialized European nations. The question in spring 1861 was how could the Confederacy maintain this critical industrial lifeline.

Onto this stage stepped Confederate Secretary of the Navy Stephen R. Mallory. Perhaps one of Jefferson Davis's better cabinet appointments, Mallory had served as the pre-war chairman of the U.S. Senate's Naval Affairs Committee and immediately recognized that the South could never match the North's superior shipbuilding capabilities unless a novel weapon was introduced into the fray. Mallory's solution was to build a fleet of ironclad vessels.

The concept of pitting "iron against wood" was not new to naval warfare. The Koreans had repulsed a Japanese invasion in 1592 with an iron-covered "tortoise ship," and during the Crimean War the French utilized floating ironclad batteries to shell Russian forts. Based on this experience in 1859, the French navy launched the *Gloire*, which was a traditional warship design covered with iron plates. The Royal Navy, not to be outdone by the French, introduced an ambitious production program. The H.M.S. *Warrior* and H.M.S. *Black Prince* were two of ten armorclads under construction in British shipyards by early 1861. Despite the European rush to build iron warships, the U.S. Navy had not made any concerted effort to construct armored vessels by the time of the Civil War.

Mallory's desire to construct Confederate blockade-breaking iron-plated steamships was given a tremendous boost when Virginia seceded from the Union. The Federals were forced to abandon Gosport Navy Yard across the Elizabeth River from Norfolk in Portsmouth. Gosport had been one of the U.S. Navy's finest navy yards, containing excellent shipbuilding facilities and materials. Of perhaps equal importance was that the retreating Federals had scuttled several ships, including the U.S.S. *Merrimack*. The Confederates then raised the *Merrimack* and began to transform the frigate into an ironclad. The effort would severely tax Southern resources; yet, it was an amazing test of Confederate ingenuity.

While the Southerners grappled with the *Merrimack*'s conversion, Union leaders also recognized the importance of building ironclads. The U.S. Navy established an ironclad board in August 1861 to review armored ship concepts. The board reluctantly selected John Ericsson's novel design as one of three vessels to be constructed in East Coast shipyards. The U.S.S. *Monitor*, initially called "Ericsson's Folly," was truly a unique vessel. Virtually awash with the sea and topped with a towering 9-foot-tall two-gun revolving turret, the ironclad was called by one crew member, "the strangest craft I had ever seen." As the Confederates slowly struggled with the *Merrimack*'s transformation, the *Monitor* was constructed in a little over 100 days. Secretary of the Navy Gideon Welles wanted the Union ironclad to quickly reach Hampton Roads to destroy the Confederate ironclad in drydock. His dreams would be shattered by a mere day.

Even though both ironclads were ready for battle by early March, the *Merrimack*, now re-christened as the C.S.S. *Virginia*, would win the race to gain naval supremacy in Hampton Roads. While the *Monitor* struggled against a gale along the mid-Atlantic coast toward the Chesapeake Capes, the Confederate ironclad ram steamed into Hampton Roads on March 8, 1862, and wreaked havoc amongst the Union fleet. The *Virginia*, impervious to Federal cannonfire, rammed and sank one ship, then shelled another into submission and left it a burning hulk. Southerners rejoiced over their great naval victory, and Northerners feared the worse.

The *Monitor*, which nearly foundered en route to the Chesapeake, entered Hampton Roads after dusk on March 8. The harbor was aglow from the burning U.S.S. *Congress*, and the *Monitor* was ordered to protect the grounded U.S.S. *Minnesota*. When the *Virginia* renewed its attack against the Federal fleet on the morning of March 9, the crew of the Confederate ironclad was shocked to see the "cheesebox on a raft" approach their ship from alongside of the *Minnesota*. During the next four hours, the *Monitor* and the *Virginia* fought each other. Neither ship could gain an advantage until a shell struck the *Monitor*'s pilothouse, blinding her commander, Lieutenant John Lorimer Worden, and causing the *Monitor* to temporarily disengage. Believing that the Federal ironclad was severely damaged, the *Virginia* steamed back to Norfolk with the receding tide.

Neither ironclad had been seriously damaged during the March 9 engagement and both claimed victory. Tactical success must be accorded to the *Monitor*, as the Union ironclad had effectively defended the *Minnesota* and the rest of the wooden Union fleet. The strategic victor, however, was the *Virginia*, as the Confederate ironclad retained control of Hampton Roads. The *Virginia*'s ability to defend Norfolk and the James River approach to Richmond altered and delayed the Federal army's attempt to strike at the Confederate capital by way of the Peninsula. Perhaps even of greater importance was the engagement's impact on naval warfare. The *Virginia*'s sinking of two wooden vessels on March 8 and the technological superiority of the *Monitor*'s iron, revolving turret in effect sank all of the world's wooden navies. Iron now ruled supreme across the seas.

One
U.S.S. MERRIMACK

The Crimean War introduced new technology that set the stage for a naval rivalry during the post-war era. The first of these new weapons was the shellgun and explosive shell developed in 1824 by General Henri J. Paixhans. A Russian squadron, armed with Paixhans's shells, demolished a Turkish wooden fleet on November 30, 1853, at Sinope on the Black Sea. The French responded to this threat by constructing iron-clad floating batteries, which provided protection necessary to attack Russian shore batteries. Based on these lessons, the French launched the iron-protected, wooden frigate *Gloire* in 1859, and the British began work on the iron-cased H.M.S. *Warrior*. The United States also sought to upgrade its navy in the mid-1850s, and Congress, despite the recommendations of the Delafield Report, which advocated the construction of ironclads, appropriated money to construct six experimental steam frigates. The first of these vessels was the U.S.S. *Merrimack* (pictured here).

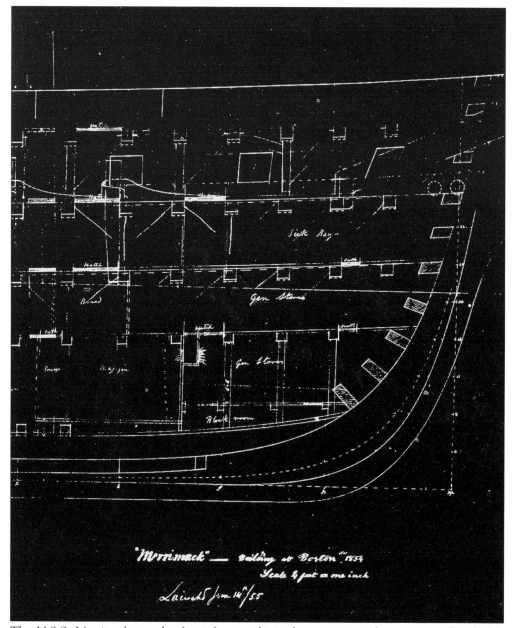

"Merrimack" — *building at Boston* 1854
Scale ½ feet to one inch
Launched June 14ᵗʰ/55

The U.S.S. *Merrimack* was the first of a new line of steam-powered, screw-propeller-driven frigates for the U.S. Navy. Perhaps the line's most notable feature was the screw-propeller. This propulsion method was designed by John Ericsson; although, some give credit to Sir Francis Pettit Smith. It enabled the warship's engines to be installed below the waterline, thereby providing protection for the propulsion unit from enemy cannon fire.

The other five ships in this class were all named in honor of American rivers: *Wabash*, *Colorado*, *Roanoke*, *Minnesota*, and *Niagara*. The *Merrimack* was named for the Merrimack River (and not the town of Merrimac). Confusion concerning the spelling of the frigate's name continues to this day. Official U.S. Navy records clearly document the vessel's name as *Merrimack*.

John Lenthall (pictured here), chief of the U.S. Bureau of Naval Construction, developed the overall concepts for the new class. Lenthall was later called by Admiral David D. Porter "the ablest naval architect in any country." His plans were completed on June 27, 1854, and forwarded to Charlestown Navy Yard near Boston. The *Merrimack*'s keel was laid on September 23, 1854. Construction was supervised by Commodore Francis Hoyt Gregory, commander of the Charlestown Navy Yard, and directed by the yard's naval constructor Edward H. Deleno. Eventually the *Merrimack* evolved into a powerful vessel displacing 3,211 tons. She was 275 feet long, had a breadth of 26 feet, 6 inches, and a draft of 23 feet. Her armament totaled 40 guns, including 24 nine-inch Dahlgrens, 2 ten-inch pivot guns, and 14 eight-inch broadside guns. The U.S. Navy recorded the vessel's cost at $685,842.19.

Over 20,000 spectators attended the *Merrimack*'s June 14, 1855 launching. Miss Mary E. Simmons, daughter of Master Carpenter Melvin Simmons, U.S.N., sponsored and christened the *Merrimack*. In tribute to the American Temperance Society (which had been founded in Boston), Miss Simmons christened the frigate with a bottle of water from the Merrimack River. A 31-gun salute, one for each state of the Union, was fired as the *Merrimack* slid down the ways and "shot out into the stream about half way to East Boston before stopping." Newspapers proclaimed the ship as a "new and important addition to our naval force."

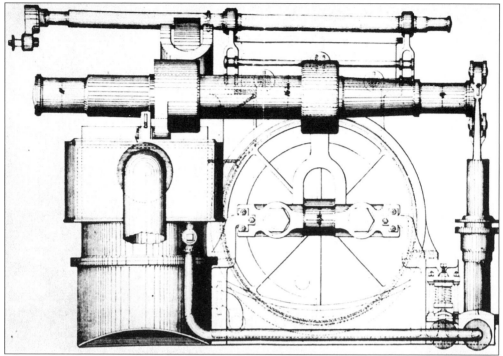

The U.S.S. *Merrimack* was commissioned on February 20, 1856, and was quickly acclaimed as the pride of the U.S. Navy. She left Boston on February 25, 1856, under the command of Captain Garrett J. Pendergrast. The frigate arrived at Annapolis on April 19 with great fanfare. President Franklin Pierce surveyed the new warship and proclaimed her "a magnificent specimen of naval architecture." The *Merrimack* returned to the Charlestown Navy Yard for refitting and then sailed for Europe. Royal Navy authorities were very impressed by the *Merrimack* when she visited British ports. They recognized the steam screw frigate as the "finest vessel of war of her class that had ever been constructed." The *Merrimack* returned to Charlestown Navy Yard on April 22, 1857, for an extensive overhaul. The frigate was re-commissioned on September 1, 1857, and sailed to the Pacific Ocean on October 17 as the flagship of Commodore John Collins Long's Pacific Squadron.

In many ways the *Merrimack* was an experimental vessel. Captain John Dahlgren, chief of the U.S. Navy Ordnance Bureau, sent his assistant, Lieutenant Catesby ap Roger Jones, on the frigate's first voyage to test its heavy cannon. Many of the new guns aboard the *Merrimack* were designed by Dahlgren. The cannon tests proved satisfactory; however, Jones noted that a "vessel with such great deadrise as the *Merrimack's* could not offer a heavy battery with substantial stability . . . In a heavy sea . . . it will be difficult to handle her battery." There were other, more serious, technical problems aboard the *Merrimack*. The engines were a constant problem. They had been designed by Robert Parrott and built at the West Point Foundry in Cold Springs, New York. The large 72-inch diameter cylinders produced 869 horsepower. Daniel B. Martin, engineer-in-chief of the U.S. Navy, designed the two huge 28-ton boilers. These brass water tube boilers were criticized for overheating and often causing the engines to race. The troublesome steam control valves malfunctioned regularly, which could lead to a total engine shutdown. Problems with the engines prompted a greater reliance on sail power. However, the sailing capabilities of the frigate were also questioned. Many observers noted that the *Merrimack's* bottom was too sharp for the ship's center of gravity and proportion of breadth. Catesby Jones commented that she "rolled very deeply—rolled badly."

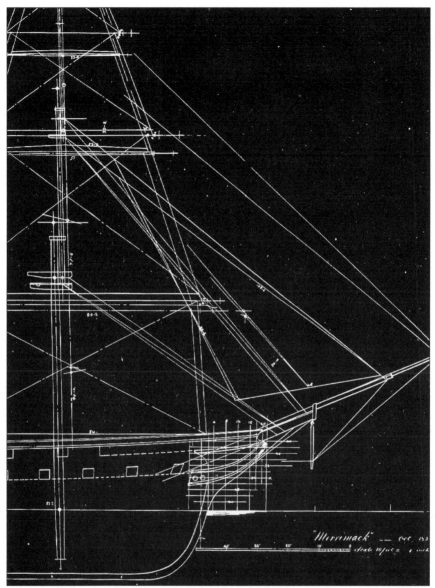

Not only were the engines unreliable, but the propeller also caused several problems. The *Merrimack* was fitted with a bronze frame system, called a banjo, to lift the propeller out of the water when the ship operated under sail. The system regularly malfunctioned due to broken parts or the engine's inability to hoist the propeller out of the water. The twin-bladed propeller weighed 13 tons and was 17 feet in diameter. It had been narrowly designed to limit drag while the frigate operated under sail. This limited surface caused excessive slippage through the water and the slow turning rate (40 r.p.m.) provided inadequate power to make headway against strong currents. The entire propulsion system was so undependable that during the *Merrimack*'s last cruise in the Pacific Ocean two of the Navy's leading engineer officers, Alban C. Stimers and H. Ashton Ramsay, were assigned to the *Merrimack*. When operating, the frigate's engine consumed 2,880 pounds of coal per hour, producing a top speed of 6 knots. It is no wonder that the *Merrimack*'s engine was described as "exclusively auxiliary to her sails, and to be used only in going in and out of port . . ."

When the U.S.S. *Merrimack* finished her Pacific Squadron service, she was ordered to Gosport Navy Yard. The *Merrimack* arrived on February 16, 1860, and was immediately placed in ordinary for an overhaul and repair of her engines. There, the frigate languished with its machinery dismantled.

Gosport Navy Yard, located across the Elizabeth River from the busy port of Norfolk, was one of the largest yards in the United States. The yard was originally a private concern founded by Loyalist Andrew Sprowle in 1767. The yard was confiscated by the Commonwealth of Virginia during the Revolutionary War and then burned by the British in 1779. The yard was leased by the United States government in 1794, and in 1798, the U.S. Navy designated it Gosport Navy Yard. It was purchased from the Commonwealth by the U.S. Navy in 1801. Captain Samuel Barron served as the first superintendent. The yard was expanded continuously throughout the nineteenth century. A large granite drydock, capable of repairing "any size ship of the line," was completed in 1837 at the cost of $1 million. By 1854, Gosport employed over 1,400 workers and its stocks, drydock, ship houses, machinery, and supplies were valued at nearly $10 million.

Gosport was indeed one of the finest shipyards in the world. The yard had gained critical acclaim for its construction of the ship of the line U.S.S. *Delaware* and two of the *Merrimack's* sister steam frigates, the *Colorado* and *Roanoke*. Numerous U.S. Navy vessels had been repaired at the yard, including the U.S.S. *Constellation* and U.S.S. *Constitution*. Gosport became one of the U.S. Navy's centers for training and testing new equipment. A diving bell apparatus was used in 1824 to repair a leak in the hull of the U.S.S. *Delaware*. The bell was also employed in the construction of a stone quay. Gun and shot testing platforms were installed. Accordingly, in 1852 several experiments were completed testing the "capacity of iron vessels in resisting the force of shells and cannon balls." The tests "proved that iron is not so invulnerable as many have heretofore supposed."

Despite all of the improvements at Gosport Navy Yard during the 1850s, the sectional crisis of 1860 found the yard in a depression. The workforce had dropped to less than 700 men and little work was accomplished. Almost a dozen ships could be found at the yard, either placed in ordinary or awaiting various types of repair. These vessels included the following: the U.S.S. *Pennsylvania*, 120 guns; the U.S.S. *Columbus*, 74 guns; the U.S.S. *Delaware*, 74 guns; the U.S.S. *New York*, 74 guns; the U.S.S. *Merrimack*, 40 guns; the U.S.S. *United States*, 50 guns; the U.S.S. *Columbia*, 50 guns; the U.S.S. *Rarilan*, 50 guns; the U.S.S. *Plymouth*, 22 guns; the U.S.S. *Germantown*, 22 guns; and the U.S.S. *Dolphin*, 4 guns. By early 1861, however, Gosport was in "disorder and confusion." Secretary of the Navy Gideon Welles ordered the U.S.S. *Cumberland*, commanded by Flag Officer Garrett J. Pendergrast and already anchored near the yard awaiting repairs, to stay in the Hampton Roads region to protect Gosport and Fort Monroe in light of the recent fall of Fort Sumter.

One reason for the confusion at Gosport Navy Yard was leadership. The problem rested squarely on the shoulders of the yard's commandant (his quarters are pictured here), Commodore Charles Stewart McCauley. McCauley had served in the U.S. Navy since he was 15 years old. He had fought in the War of 1812, and his long career included command of both the Pacific and South Atlantic Squadrons. During the Mexican War, McCauley commanded the Washington Navy Yard and when he was appointed commandant of Gosport Navy Yard in 1860, it appeared to be a wise choice. The 67-year-old McCauley, however, was rumored to have taken to drink and often ridiculed for being too old for active command. Under orders to "do nothing to upset the Virginians" during the tense days of April 1861, many would question his decision-making abilities.

President Abraham Lincoln's call for 75,000 volunteers, following the fall of Fort Sumter, to suppress the Southern rebellion prompted Virginia to secede from the Union on April 17, 1861. Hampton Roads immediately became a major flashpoint. Virginians clamored to secure Federal property, which they believed to rightly belong to the Commonwealth. Fort Monroe on Old Point Comfort, Fort Calhoun on the Rip Raps in the middle of Hampton Roads, and Gosport Navy Yard in Portsmouth were military assets that the North and South wished to control. The two forts seemed out of Virginia's reach, but Gosport appeared ripe for conquest.

Gideon Welles (pictured here) had already taken steps to retrieve the *Merrimack* from Gosport. On April 10, 1861, he ordered Commodore McCauley to get the *Merrimack* ready to steam to Philadelphia "or in case of danger from unlawful attempts to take possession of her, that she should be placed beyond their reach." Welles further advised that McCauley should "exercise . . . judgment in discharging the responsibility that rests upon you." Gosport's commandant responded by telegram that it would take a month to revitalize the *Merrimack*'s dismantled engines. Welles replied by sending U.S. Navy Engineer-in-Chief Benjamin F. Isherwood to Portsmouth to repair the *Merrimack*'s engines. Isherwood arrived at Gosport Navy Yard on April 14, 1861, and immediately set to work around the clock restoring the frigate's machinery. The emergency repairs were completed on April 17, and Isherwood proudly reported to the yard commandant that the *Merrimack* would be ready to leave port the next day. On the morning of April 18, Isherwood had steam in the ship's boilers and the jury-rigged engines seemed capable of taking the *Merrimack* at least as far as the protection of Fort Monroe. McCauley, however, advised Isherwood and the *Merrimack*'s commander, Commander James Alden, that he had decided to retain the frigate in port. Alden and Isherwood pleaded with McCauley, but to no avail. The *Merrimack*'s fires were banked and the two officers left for Washington to explain to Secretary Welles why the frigate had not left Gosport.

McCauley's indecision was caused by several factors. The yard commandant's actions were tempered by his interpretation of Welles's command "that there should be no steps taken to give needless alarm." His decisions, or lack thereof, were further influenced by the many pro-Southern officers on his staff (13 of 20 would later serve the Confederacy). McCauley planned to use the U.S.S. *Cumberland*, recently moved up the Elizabeth River from the Portsmouth Naval Hospital to a position just off Gosport. The Federals could then utilize the sloop's firepower to either effectively defend the yard or to release ships, such as the *Merrimack*, so that they could be transferred to safer havens. Instead, McCauley found excuses for inaction everywhere and was passive as events headed toward an explosive conclusion.

As the Federals struggled with McCauley's procrastination, local Southern patriots were quickly organizing their own effort to secure Gosport Navy Yard. A "Vigilant Committee" was established while militia troops mustered in Norfolk and Portsmouth. Fort Norfolk was seized and with it a very useful powder magazine. Batteries were rapidly constructed along the Elizabeth River, and several ships were sunk in the channel off Sewell's Point to block Union access to the navy yard. The obstructions, primarily consisting of three light ships, were considered by Commander James Alden, U.S.N., to be insufficient to halt any Federal ship traffic. Nevertheless, the pro-Southern citizenry was in a bellicose mood and gathered outside the yard's gates shouting that Gosport should be handed over to the Commonwealth of Virginia.

Several Virginia militia officers, including William Booth Taliaferro (pictured here seated), Henry Heth, and William Mahone (all destined to become Confederate generals), arrived in Portsmouth and opened negotiations with Commodore McCauley. Taliaferro, a Mexican War veteran and former member of the House of Delegates, advised McCauley that he planned to assume possession of Gosport Navy Yard on behalf of the Sovereign State of Virginia. Virginia's dignity demanded nothing less. When McCauley refused to concede, Taliaferro telegraphed for more troops to be sent to Portsmouth from South Carolina so that Gosport could be taken by assault. Then Taliaferro began running trains in and out of Portsmouth to give the impression that his command was increasing by the hour.

When the *Merrimack* failed to leave Gosport Navy Yard on April 18, Gideon Welles realized that more resolute action was required. Welles dispatched Commodore Hiram Paulding, a veteran of 50 years of naval service, on board the 8-gun steamer U.S.S. *Pawnee* with 100 marines to take command at Gosport and protect all United States property in the yard. Paulding reached Fort Monroe on the afternoon of April 20 and embarked 350 men of the Third Massachusetts Volunteer Infantry Regiment. He arrived at Gosport around 8 p.m., but Paulding was too late. McCauley had finally taken decisive action and begun scuttling the warships at Gosport.

Paulding assumed command from a demoralized McCauley, but quickly realized that there was little else that he could do other than finish the job that McCauley had initiated. Elements of the Third Massachusetts guarded the yard's outer walls so that the angry mob outside the gates would not attempt to disrupt the work of demolition crews. As an extra precaution, the *Cumberland* and *Pawnee* were anchored in the Elizabeth River to enable their cannons to rake the approaches to the yard. The local Southern patriots could only observe from afar the flames' destructive work.

Union crews immediately went forward with their assigned demolition tasks. Paulding had stocked the *Pawnee* with a wide variety of combustibles, including 40 barrels of gun powder, 11 tanks of turpentine, 12 barrels of cotton waste, and 181 flares, to destroy the yard. The mighty 140-gun *Pennsylvania*, now engulfed in a mass of flames, dominated the eerie scene. No one had unloaded the ship's cannon, so the night was filled with occasional blasts from the 4-decker's guns. Since everything would not burn, seamen and marines rushed through the yard laying powder trails to destroy the valuable machinery and facilities. There were over 1,200 cannon in the yard, including 300 new Dahlgrens. When efforts to break off the trunnions with sledgehammers proved futile, the guns were spiked with wrought-iron nails. Two officers, Commander John Rodgers and Captain H.G. Wright, were assigned the important task of mining the granite drydock. Their work was purportedly foiled by a petty officer who did not wish the explosion to damage the nearby homes of his pre-war friends.

At 4:20 a.m., Paulding ordered his men to the ships. The tide was rising and everything that could be done to destroy the yard's military value, he thought, had been done. The men raced back to the ships, lighting the final fires behind them. As the evening sky turned bright by the flames, the *Pawnee* steamed out of the harbor, followed by the *Cumberland* under tow by the gunboat *Yankee*.

The small Union flotilla slowly made its way down the Elizabeth River past the feared, but non-existent Confederate batteries. The Federal ships crossed the obstructions sunk in the channel by Southern volunteers before dawn. "We were dragged over the obstruction," remembered Lieutenant Selfridge of the U.S.S. *Cumberland*, "and anchored off Fort Monroe." The *Cumberland* immediately became the nucleus of the Federal squadron blockading Hampton Roads and the lower Chesapeake Bay.

The entire operation was over by 6:15 a.m., and only two men were lost by the U.S. Navy. Commander John Rodgers and Captain H.G. Wright failed to reach the retreating Federal ships and were captured by Taliaferro's troops. The Confederates, however, gained in one evening one of the finest shipyards in America.

Two
TRANSFORMATION

When the Virginia volunteers entered Gosport Navy Yard the morning after the blaze, evidence of destruction was everywhere. Nevertheless, amongst all the rubble, scuttled ships, and charred buildings, the Confederacy was able to find the wherewithal to create a challenge to the U.S. Navy.

"The condition of the Navy Yard at Portsmouth as it appeared on the 21st and 22nd was melancholy to look upon," wrote Paymaster William H. Peters of the Virginia State Navy in his inventory of the yard following its abandonment by the Federals. "It was a mass of ruins. The extensive row of buildings on the north front of the yard which contained large quantities of manufactured articles and valuable materials was totally destroyed, together with their contents." The yard appeared, at first glance, devastated. Ship Houses "A" and "B" were burned, and the ship of the line U.S.S. *New York* was nothing but smoldering timbers. Out in the Elizabeth River, all of the ships, except for the venerable U.S.S. *United States*, were either scuttled or burned.

The Federals left with such haste that their destructive work was far from complete. Much of the property was still intact. Over five warehouses filled with naval supplies, including $56,269 worth of clothing and $38,763 in food, survived the flames. The Federals also abandoned a tremendous array of ordnance, including 1,085 heavy cannon and 250,000 pounds of powder. Numerous dwellings, the foundry, machine shop, and several workshops remained untouched by the blaze. More importantly, the retreating Federals failed to destroy the granite drydock. Overnight, the Confederacy gained the infrastructure to construct the vessels to challenge the Federal blockade. The Richmond press gloated over the abundance of equipment and supplies stating, "we have material enough to build a navy of iron-plated ships."

Captain Robert Pegram of the Virginia State Navy assumed command of Gosport Navy Yard for the Commonwealth of Virginia on April 20, 1861. Pegram was replaced on April 22 by the 50-year naval veteran Flag Officer French Forrest. Forrest (pictured here) was known as a "blusterer of the real old-tar school," and he energetically set himself to the immense task of reorganizing the yard. Buildings were repaired, the Naval Hospital reopened, and shops revitalized. Forrest even sent divers to investigate several of the hulls lying beneath the Elizabeth River. Thus, when the Commonwealth officially transferred the yard to the Confederacy on May 30, it was already humming with activity.

Forrest also recognized the virtual defenseless state of Norfolk and Portsmouth. Elements of the Federal fleet, including the U.S.S. *Cumberland*, were anchored in Hampton Roads, and the Union had retained control of Fort Monroe and the Rip Raps battery. Major General Benjamin Franklin Butler, commander of the Union Department of Virginia, had occupied and fortified Newport News Point on May 27, 1861. Camp Butler's 8-inch Columbiads controlled the entrance to the James River, hindering the Confederate transportation link between Norfolk and Richmond. Forrest sought to counter this Union threat with the construction of earthworks along the southside of Hampton Roads. The yard commandant utilized 196 heavy guns captured at Gosport to arm batteries at strategic sites such as Sewell's Point, Craney Island, and Pig Point.

Union gunboats tested the Confederate fortifications on several occasions, as depicted in this May 1861 scene of the gunboat *Yankee* shelling the Craney Island battery. The Federals learned that the Confederate heavy ordnance provided Norfolk and Portsmouth ample protection against any naval attack. A stalemate existed between Union and Confederate forces poised on either side of Hampton Roads.

Meanwhile, Flag Officer Forrest contracted the B & I Baker Wrecking Company on May 18, 1861, to raise the *Merrimack*. Even though Forrest felt that the operation was a poor use of resources, he reported to Robert E. Lee on May 30, "We have the *Merrimack* up and just pulling her in the dry dock." While questions were raised regarding what to do with this "burned and blackened hulk," Forrest also arranged for Baker Company to raise the two scuttled sloops of war, *Germantown* and *Plymouth*.

Gosport Navy Yard's capture was a godsend for the agrarian South. Since the Union blockade strangled Southern trade, Gosport provided the Confederacy with the capability to build ships to challenge the Union fleet. The man who truly recognized Gosport's ability to achieve this goal was Confederate Secretary of the Navy Stephen Russell Mallory. Perhaps one of Jefferson Davis's better cabinet appointments, Mallory was born in 1812 in Trinidad and moved to Key West, Florida, when he was a young boy. Well educated, he became inspector of customs at Key West when 19 years old. He became a lawyer in 1839, served as a local judge, and rose to political prominence. Mallory was elected senator in 1851 and in 1854 and became chairman of the Committee on Naval Affairs. While serving as a committee chairman, Mallory worked to modernize the U.S. Navy. He was successful obtaining appropriations to construct new screw-propeller steam frigates and sloops of war, which became the envy of European navies. Mallory's efforts to champion the construction of an iron-cased battery, designed by Robert L. Stevens for the defense of New York Harbor, proved unsuccessful. His tenure as chairman of the Committee on Naval Affairs prepared him to assume the tremendous task of creating a navy from nothing.

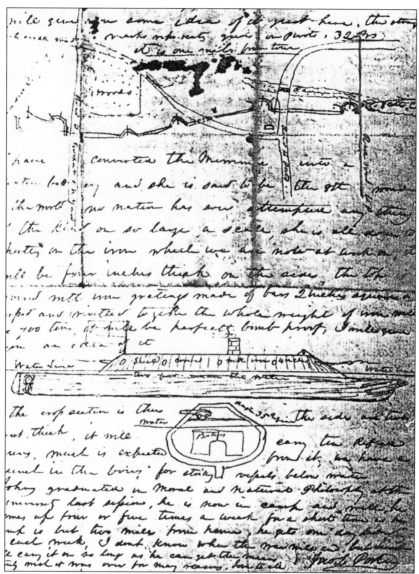

Mallory immediately recognized upon assuming the duties of secretary of the navy that the Confederacy required a new type of warship to challenge the Union Navy. He advised the Confederate Congress the following:

I regard the possession of an iron-armored ship as a matter of the first necessity. Such a vessel at this time could traverse the entire coast of the United States, prevent all blockades, and encounter, with a fair prospect of success, their entire Navy.

If to cope with them upon the sea we follow their example and build wooden ships, we shall have to construct several at one time; for one or two ships would fall an easy prey to her comparatively numerous steam frigates. But inequality of numbers may be compensated by invulnerability; and thus not only does economy but naval success dictate the wisdom and expediency of fighting with iron against wood, without regard to first cost.

27

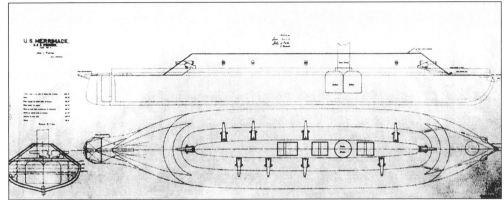

The *Merrimack*, now in drydock at Gosport, appeared to be the best solution for Mallory to implement an ironclad construction program. Consequently, Mallory held a meeting in Richmond on June 23, 1861, to review and plan the *Merrimack*'s conversion. Lieutenant John Mercer Brooke, Naval Constructor John Luke Porter, and Chief Engineer William Price Williamson formed a committee to plan and execute the *Merrimack*'s transformation into an ironclad. Porter had actually brought with him a model of an iron-cased floating harbor-defense battery he had created in 1848, while Brooke provided drawings he had just made at Mallory's request. Both designs featured an inclined casemate, but Brooke's concept submerged the bow and stern of the vessel to enhance buoyancy and speed. Since Mallory unrealistically wanted an ocean-going armored warship, Brooke's design became the plan selected for the *Merrimack*'s conversion.

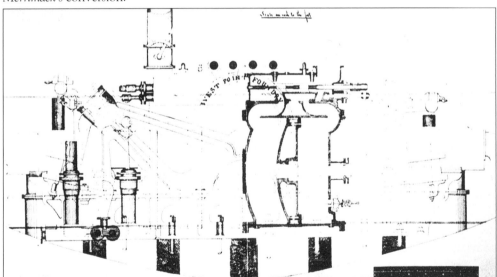

Even before Mallory gained formal approval from the Confederate Congress, work commenced on the *Merrimack*'s reconfiguration. As Porter supervised the cutting away of the *Merrimack*'s charred timbers, Brooke and Williamson sought to solve the power plant problems. They quickly learned that new engines provided by Tredegar Iron Works in Richmond would take too long to build. Chief Engineer Williamson decided that the old, previously condemned engines of the *Merrimack* could be reworked despite serious corrosion from the saltwater of the Elizabeth River. Williamson was fortunate that he could rely on the services of G. Ashton Ramsay to revitalize the engines. Ramsay had served on the *Merrimack* before the war and knew "her every timber by heart."

Mallory, an astute politician, presented his request for a project appropriation to the Confederate Congress. He reported that reconstruction of the *Merrimack* as a frigate would cost $450,000, but the conversion to an armorclad would cost only $172,523. The ironclad project was approved. Despite that shrewd success, Mallory did error with his shipbuilding program; he delegated responsibilities among several individuals. French Forrest, who did not really approve of the project, retained administrative control as yard commandant, Chief Engineer William Williamson was given the task of machinery revitalization, and Naval Constructor John L. Porter was charged with supervising the actual construction. John Mercer Brooke managed the armor and armament for the ironclad as well as acting as Mallory's inspecting officer for the entire project. Friction arose immediately between Brooke and Porter since much of the project overlapped. The acrimony began with the fact that both men claimed the vessel's design as their own. Brooke was a favorite of Mallory, and the secretary eventually would assign credit to Brooke. Lieutenant John Mercer Brooke (pictured here) was perhaps one of the most inventive minds in the Confederate Navy. Brooke was born in 1825 in Tampa, Florida, and graduated from the U.S. Naval Academy at Annapolis in 1847. His career was filled with success, including the invention of a bathometer, which won the Gold Medal of Science from the Academy of Berlin.

Naval Constructor John L. Porter would actually complete all of the construction plans for the conversion. Porter was a Portsmouth native whose naval career had not been as successful as Brooke's. He failed his first examination for a U.S. Navy constructors appointment. After passing the test ten years later, Porter was tried for neglect of duty in 1860 concerning the construction of the U.S.S. *Seminole*. Though Porter was acquitted, he remained embittered. Nevertheless, he was the only naval constructor to join the Confederacy. Despite his faults and problems with Brooke, Porter immersed himself in his work on the *Merrimack*. Porter supervised the removal of all of the upper works and then cut the vessel on a straight line from bow to stern at the berth deck level. The main gun deck was laid, and the casemate began to take shape. Porter's plan called for a length of just over 262 feet and a draft of 21 feet.

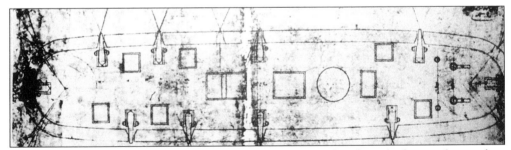

The casemate was the ironclad's most distinctive feature, 28 feet from the bow and extending aft 172 feet. The fantail continued another 56 feet. The sides were sloped upward at a 36-degree angle to deflect shot. This acute slope allowed only 7 feet of headroom and a beam of 30 feet, which forced the cannons to be staggered along the opposing broadside to accommodate recoil. The roof was grated to provide ventilation to the gun deck. The grating was manufactured of 2-inch iron bars supporting rafters of yellow pine and white oak. Three hatchways were constructed to enable access to the 14-foot-wide deck. At the front of the casemate was a 12-inch-thick iron conical pilothouse.

The casemate was constructed of 4 inches of oak laid horizontally, 8 inches of yellow pine laid vertically, and 12 inches of white pine laid horizontally. It was bolted together and then eventually sheathed with 2-inch-thick 2-by-6-inch iron plate laid horizontally. A second course of similar iron plate covered the first layer vertically. The deck, designed to be almost awash with the sea, was covered with 1 inch of iron plate. An additional course of 1-inch iron plate extended 3 feet from the deck to a depth of 3 feet around the vessel. The joining of the casemate to the hull was an obvious weak point. Porter had devised the displacement that would submerge the knuckle 2 feet below the waterline. The casemate eaves were also extended 2 feet to provide additional protection from shot aimed at the ironclad's hull.

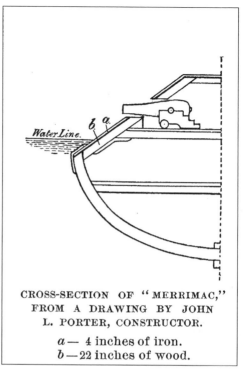

CROSS-SECTION OF "MERRIMAC," FROM A DRAWING BY JOHN L. PORTER, CONSTRUCTOR.

a — 4 inches of iron.
b — 22 inches of wood.

Brooke also worked with Tredegar Iron Works on the production of rifled cannon as part of his effort to arm the *Merrimack*. He developed a brilliant system of converting old smoothbore cannon into rifles by forging bands over their breech to resist the greater pressure of firing rifled projectiles. Brooke invented special explosive shells and, more importantly, an elongated armor-piercing, wrought-iron bolt for both the 7-inch and 6.4-inch versions of his rifled cannon. Since Mallory wanted the *Merrimack* armed with the finest heavy cannon, Tredegar immediately forged ahead with the production of Brooke's rifles and projectiles. Thus, Brooke proposed that the *Merrimack* be armed with a broadside battery of six 9-inch Dahlgren smoothbores and two 6.4-inch rifles. Two of the Dahlgrens were hot-shot guns. At each end of the casemate, three gun ports were pierced for the two 7-inch Brooke rifles, which served as pivot guns.

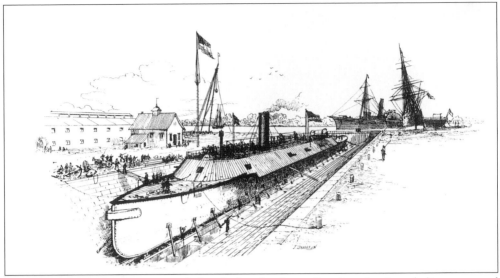

John Mercer Brooke was assigned the dual task of coordinating the ironclad's armor and armament. He stayed in Richmond to supervise the production of iron plate by Tredegar Iron Works. The initial contract, based on Porter's specifications, called for 1-inch-thick, 8-foot-long iron plate. Tredegar had adequate facilities to produce this size plate, and within a week of the July 24, 1861 contract, the firm was ready to ship plates to Gosport. Brooke, however, was uncertain that three courses of 1-inch plate would provide the casemate with adequate shot-proof qualities. Consequently, Brooke and Catesby ap Roger Jones conducted tests on Jamestown Island. Using rifled cannon and projectiles designed by Brooke, they penetrated the 3-inch plate test shield at 300 yards. This forced Tredegar to re-tool its plate-rolling capacity to produce the necessary 2-inch plate. Even when the plates were completed, there were difficulties and delays transporting the iron from Richmond to Gosport Navy Yard. Tredegar completed its plate production on February 12, 1862. Production totaled 723 tons, at a cost of $123,715.

The stern and bow pivot gun ports were just one of the many disagreements that arose between Brooke and Porter. Porter had overlooked this opportunity to enhance the ironclad's field of fire, and Brooke, as the project's inspecting officer and a confidant of Mallory, insisted on this improvement. The ram was another issue that only increased the animosity between the two men. Porter did not entirely approve of the 1,500-pound cast-iron ram, but installed it only at Brooke's insistence. One flange securing the ram was cracked during its mounting. Nothing was done to correct the problem. While they compromised on hatchways, Porter later wrote, "Lieut. Brooke constantly proposing alterations in her and as constantly and firmly [they were] opposed by myself." Nevertheless, most of Brooke's suggestions were valuable improvements. Brooke ordered that the steering chains be moved in an iron channel to protect the mechanism from jamming or damage from shot.

Porter was not only overworked from his responsibilities with the *Merrimack*, but also from providing designs for other Confederate shipbuilding projects. "I received but little encouragement from anyone," Porter complained, "Hundreds—I may say thousands—asserted she would never float." Delays caused by construction problems, technical agreements, and delivery of iron plate from Richmond plagued the conversion project. Many observers wondered if the project would ever be completed, as the executive officer of Gosport asked, "do you really think she will float?" Mallory's concerns about the project prompted him to assign the 40-year-old Virginia native Lieutenant Catesby ap Roger Jones as the *Merrimack*'s executive officer in November 1861. Jones was a noted U.S. Navy ordnance expert and had served aboard the U.S.S. *Merrimack* during the frigate's maiden voyage. David Dixon Porter wrote that Jones and Brooke were a loss for the Union Navy. Jones's early assignment to the *Merrimack* expedited construction, in part, by mitigating the disagreements between Brooke and Porter. His further duties included mounting the ironclad's ordnance, mustering a crew, and preparing the vessel for sea. Jones (pictured here) had numerous problems to resolve. The conversion project was scheduled for completion in late November, but it was not until late January that the ironclad was finished.

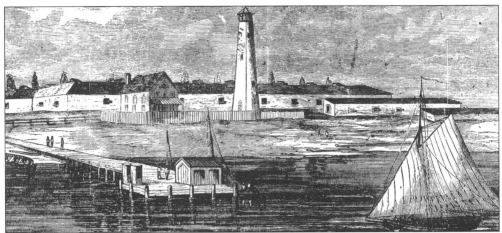

The Confederates were in a rush to finish the ironclad. News of the construction of several ironclads in the North, particularly "Ericsson's Battery," meant that the South might lose its naval advantage if their ironclad was not quickly put into action. Each Federal squadron that arrived in Hampton Roads was reason for alarm. Many Confederates feared that Union troops would attempt to capture Norfolk. The Federals, in turn, were extremely worried about the impending sortie of the *Merrimack*. Major General John Ellis Wool, commander of the Union Department of Virginia at Fort Monroe, continuously bombarded Washington with news of the Confederate ironclad. Wool wrote on October 17, 1861, that he had "reliable information with regard to the preparation of the *Merrimack* for an attack on Newport News . . . she will in all probability prove to be extremely formidable." He requested troop and navy support to defend the Union's toehold in Hampton Roads.

The Confederates were very concerned about security. Information leaked daily to the Federals across Hampton Roads. Escaped slaves, exchanged prisoners of war, Northern sympathizers, and other informants kept the Federals well informed about the Confederate ironclad project. Norfolk was the exchange point for civilians traveling North and South (as depicted in this engraving), which increased the flow of information. Southern newspapers were another problem. The *Mobile Register* wrote often about the *Merrimack*'s reconfiguration, proudly proclaiming that "We hope soon to hear that she is ready to commence her avenging career on the seas."

34

Nevertheless, the *Merrimack*'s conversion did not proceed as planned. Even though workmen labored seven days a week, many without an increase in pay, until eight each evening, delays continued. Jones stated to Brooke on January 24, 1862, "someone ought to be hung." The ironclad's executive officer was especially dismayed over several critical errors made by Porter, which were discovered once the vessel was afloat. Porter had miscalculated the vessel's displacement, which caused the ship to ride too high in the water. Ballast was added to lower the ironclad into the water, but this did not satisfy Jones. He wrote the following:

> The ship will be too light, or I should say, she is not sufficiently protected below the water . . . The eaves of the roof will be more than six inches immersed, which in smooth water would not be enough; a slight ripple would leave it bare except the 1-inch iron that extends some feet below. We are least protected where we most need it. The constructor should have put on six inches where now we have one.

Other problems plagued the preparations. Neither the port shutters nor the Brooke bolts had arrived from Richmond.

Jones had difficulty obtaining an adequate crew to man the ironclad. He was able to assemble an excellent group of officers, including Robert Minor, Hunter Davidson, John Taylor Wood, and G. Ashton Ramsay among others, but most of the available seamen in the South joined the Confederate Army at the war's beginning. Jones detached Lieutenant John Taylor Wood in January 1862 to search for recruits from nearby army commands. Wood met with Major General John Bankhead Magruder, commander of the Army of the Peninsula, to obtain volunteers. Magruder, who also needed more troops to man his Peninsula defensive lines, acquiesced to Wood's request and provided 200 volunteers. Wood selected 80, including Private Richard Curtis, Company A (Wythe Rifles), 32nd Virginia Volunteer Infantry Regiment, who is pictured here. His pre-war occupation was listed as boatman.

Several units from Major General Benjamin Huger's Department of Norfolk command volunteered to serve on the ironclad. One private of the 41st Virginia, Isaac Walling, a professional diver, assisted the Baker Wrecking Company in raising the *Merrimack* from the bottom of the Elizabeth River. Another private, William Duncan, had previously deserted to sail on a privateer, which never left port. He was returned to his unit only to transfer to the *Merrimack*. Over 31 men from the 41st eventually volunteered to serve on the ironclad. United Artillery (Co. E) transferred from duty at Fort Norfolk to the *Merrimack*. Captain Thomas Kevill (pictured here) and Lieutenant Edward Lakin both commanded gun crews on the ironclad.

Yard Commandant French Forrest was charged with the responsibility of securing sufficient oil, coal, and gunpowder for the *Merrimack*. Forrest had to beg, borrow, or trade for these necessary supplies from every conceivable source. Oil was obtained from a Union barge that had run aground during a storm. Even though the old, cantankerous engines consumed coal at an excessive rate, only 150 tons were loaded. This helped lower the ironclad even further in the water and compensate for Porter's miscalculations. Gunpowder proved to be the most difficult resource to procure. While 18,000 pounds were required to adequately prepare the ship for battle, only 1,000 pounds had been received from Richmond by late February. Forrest requisitioned powder from the receiving ship *Confederate States* (formerly the U.S.S. *United States*), but obtained most of the gunpowder from supplies the flag officer had transferred to Fort Norfolk (pictured here) and other batteries under Huger's command.

The *Merrimack* still lacked a captain. Mallory knew the man he wanted for the command—Franklin Buchanan. Yet, he hesitated to name him the ship's captain because of the time-honored seniority system, which placed two men, French Forrest and Victor Randolph, senior to Buchanan. Forrest actively sought the position, and Catesby Jones was "actually oppressed with the undue expectations" of being named the ironclad's commander. Both men would be disappointed. Mallory side-stepped the issue by naming Buchanan commander of the James River defenses. His flagship, of course, would be the *Merrimack*. Buchanan was an excellent choice for command of the ironclad.

A Maryland native and grandson of a signer of the Declaration of Independence, Buchanan was born September 17, 1800. He was appointed midshipman in the U.S. Navy in January 1815. Franklin Buchanan was the first superintendent of the U.S. Naval Academy and during the Mexican War commanded the sloop *Germantown* during the Siege of Vera Cruz. He was the commander of Matthew C. Perry's flagship, the U.S.S. *Susquehanna*, when Perry opened Japan to American trade. Promoted to the rank of captain in 1855, Buchanan (fondly known as "Old Buck") commanded the Washington Navy Yard when the Civil War erupted. When it appeared that Maryland would leave the Union following the April 19, 1861 Baltimore Riot, Buchanan resigned his commission. Since Maryland did not secede, Buchanan strove for reinstatement, only to be denied by Gideon Welles. Buchanan was then named a captain in the C.S. Navy and assigned to the Office of Orders and Detail until detached to prepare the Confederate ironclad for combat.

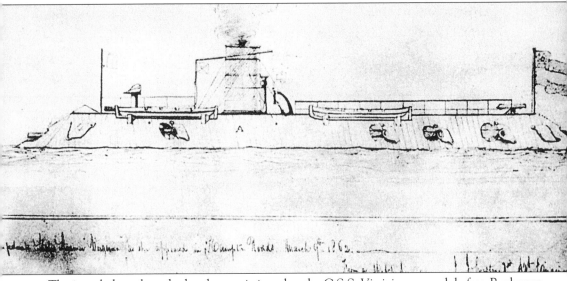

The ironclad was launched and commissioned as the C.S.S. *Virginia* one week before Buchanan assumed command. The February 17, 1862 event was an unimpressive affair. Workmen were still feverously completing the conversion and the mood was one of desperation. On March 4, 1862, however, Buchanan reported that the ironclad was ready for combat. Mallory was overjoyed. He expected great things of both Buchanan and the *Virginia*. Mallory's orders to Buchanan included his hopes for the ironclad's use, "The *Virginia* is a novelty in naval construction, is untried and her power unknown . . . Her powers as a ram are regarded as formidable, and it is hoped that you may be able to test them. Like the bayonet charge of infantry, this mode of attack, while the most distinctive, will commend itself to you in the present scarcity of ammunition. It is one also that may be rendered destructive at night against the enemy at anchor." Mallory added that "without guns the ship would be formidable as a ram."

The Confederate Secretary of the Navy suggested that if the ironclad could "pass Old Point [meaning Fort Monroe] and make a dashing cruise on the Potomac as far as Washington, its effect upon the public mind would be important to our cause." Such a bold move could surely bring victory at a time when the Confederacy was reeling from defeats in Tennessee and along the North Carolina Sounds, and Mallory was convinced "that the opportunity and the means for striking a blow for our Navy are now for the first time presented, I congratulate you upon it, and know that your judgment and gallantry will meet all just expectations." Mallory concluded his letter stating that "Action, prompt and successful action—now would be of serious importance to our cause." The portrait at the left is of Douglas French Forrest, son of Gosport Navy Yard commandant French Forrest and volunteer aide to Franklin Buchanan.

Three
ERICSSON'S FOLLY

When Gosport Navy Yard fell into the hands of the Confederacy, many Northern naval leaders thought the Confederacy could not use the demolished yard and scuttled ships. Flag Officer Silas Horton Stringham, commander of the North Atlantic Blockading Squadron, advised that the *Merrimack* was "pronounced worthless. Her machinery was all destroyed." Despite Lieutenant H.A. Wise's boast that the frigate was "consumed to a mere hull," rumors persisted throughout summer 1861 that the Confederates had embarked on the *Merrimack*'s conversion into an ironclad. The concept of creating armor-clad vessels capable of countering any ironclad the South might produce was not lost upon Secretary of the Navy Gideon Welles. Welles, a former newspaper owner and Democrat who served in the Navy Department before joining the Republican party in 1855, recognized that the U.S. Navy was outdated and needed a sound shipbuilding program.

Welles advised Congress that "much attention has been given within the last few years to the subject of floating batteries, or steamers," and recommended "the appointment of a proper and competent board to enquire into the matter." Congress appropriated $1.5 million for the construction of armor-clad warships and authorized the appointment of an Ironclad Board to review designs. President Lincoln signed the bill into law on August 3, 1861. Commodores Joseph Smith (pictured here) and Hiram Paulding and Captain Charles Henry Davis were appointed to serve on the board and to select one to three prototype vessels for construction. Welles immediately solicited bids, and by early September 1861, the board had received 16 proposals, of which two were selected. Merrick and Sons of Philadelphia proposed constructing a European-styled ironclad, which would eventually be named *New Ironsides*. The other selection was a design submitted by Cornelius S. Bushnell and would be known as the *Galena*.

The Ironclad Board, however, questioned whether the *Galena* was seaworthy. Bushnell, an affluent businessman who dabbled in railroads, shipbuilding, wholesaling, and politics, knew little about the vessel's design and sought counsel. Cornelius Delameter, a leading New York iron founder, advised Bushnell to seek out Swedish engineer John Ericsson for advice. During this meeting, Ericsson explained why the *Galena* was seaworthy, and he also showed Bushnell his model of a floating battery design that had been offered to France during the Crimean War. Bushnell recognized the brilliance of the concept and offered to promote his naval design. Bushnell reviewed the concept with Gideon Welles, who wrote in his diary that the ironclad was "extraordinary and valuable." The Ironclad Board was not as impressed. Captain Davis (pictured here) could not imagine such a warship and told Bushnell to "Take the little boat home and worship it as it would not be idolatry, because it was in the image of nothing in the heaven above or on the earth beneath or in the waters under the earth."

Once the Ironclad Board members realized that the novel design Bushnell was promoting belonged to John Ericsson, they ridiculed the concept as another of "Ericsson's Follies." Ericsson began his career as an ordnance expert in the Swedish Army, but resigned his commission and moved to England. Even though he invented several improvements in locomotives and naval guns, his business failures resulted in Ericsson landing in debtors' prison. He immigrated to the United States and achieved acclaim with his invention of the screw propeller. Ericsson's bad relationship with the U.S. Navy dated back to the U.S.S. *Princeton* fiasco. The *Princeton* featured an engine, screw propeller, and a heavy cannon designed by Ericsson. It was a huge success until one of its 12-inch guns (not of Ericsson's design) exploded killing Secretary of State Abel P. Upshur, Secretary of the Navy T.W. Gilmer, and several other leading officials. Ericsson was blamed for the incident and labored several years to obtain payment from the Navy for his work on the *Princeton*.

Despite the board's distrust of Ericsson, Bushnell was committed to obtaining a contract to construct the ironclad. Bushnell's friendship with Gideon Welles enabled him to share the ironclad design with President Abraham Lincoln. Lincoln was impressed by Ericsson's model, commenting, "All I have to say is what the girl said when she stuck her foot into the stocking. It strikes me there's something in it."

41

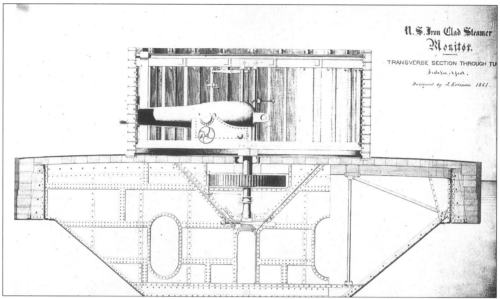

The Ironclad Board, particularly Davis, was still not convinced. Bushnell realized that his only hope for success was to urge Ericsson to explain his novel craft personally to the board. He convinced Ericsson that the board liked his concept, but that the inventor needed to travel to Washington to thoroughly describe the ship's unique features. Ericsson agreed. On September 15, 1861, Ericsson appeared at the Ironclad Board meeting and, after a few questions, was told that his plan was rejected. He asked and his retort "thrilled every person present in your room," Bushnell later recounted to Welles, "with his vivid description of what the little boat would be and what she could do." Ericsson concluded his presentation with the comment, "Gentlemen, after what I have said, I consider it to be your duty to the country to give me an order to build the vessel before I leave this room." The entire board agreed.

Ericsson promptly went to work on the project. He knew that he needed time because Gideon Welles insisted on a 90-day delivery date once the contract was signed. The inventor also realized that he needed money to put the ironclad's construction into motion. Thus, a syndicate was formed, including Ericsson, Cornelius Bushnell, Congressman John A. Griswold (pictured here), and John Winslow. These men signed a U.S. Navy contract on October 4, 1861, to build, at a cost of $275,000, an "Iron-Clad Shot-Proof Steam battery . . . with the length to be one hundred and seventy-nine feet, extreme breadth forty-one feet and a depth of five feet." Ericsson's past troubles with the U.S. Navy still haunted him, according to his contract:

> Should the vessel fail in performance for speed, sea service, failure of the turret or safety of the vessel, the men of the party of the first part hereby bid themselves, their heirs, . . . to refund to the United States the amount of money advanced to them on said vessel.

Ericsson's genius was evident in virtually every aspect of the project. He selected his partners not only for their wealth and political influence, but also for their business connections. If Ericsson was to fulfill the contract's three-month construction time line, then he needed to subcontract many of the ironclad's components to various firms. John Griswold's firm of Rensselaer Iron Works in Troy, New York, would make rivets and the bar iron for the pilothouse. The Albany Iron Works, owned by John Winslow, would provide angle iron for the ship's frame as well as some of the iron plate. Iron plate was also ordered from S. Holdane and Company of New York and the largest rolling mill in the United States, H. Abbott and Sons of Baltimore. Even though Abbott was the best equipped mill in the nation, it could only produce 1-inch plate rather than the 4-inch plate specified for the turret. Due to time constraints, Ericsson compromised on eight bands of 1-inch plate for the turret.

The ironclad itself was built at Continental Iron Works of Greenpoint in Brooklyn. The New York City firm of Novelty Iron Works, located across the East River from Greenpoint, was contracted to build the ironclad's turret. The Delameter Ironworks, located near Novelty Iron Works, received the important job of building the vessel's engines. Cornelius Delameter, owner of the firm, was Ericsson's business partner and most trusted friend. The power plant consisted of two "vibrating lever" engines designed by Ericsson and two Martin boilers. All of the machinery was located in the hull below and behind the turret chamber. A watertight bulkhead separated the two sections, providing an airtight seal. The required air supply was brought into the engine compartment via a forced draft system using two large deck airtakes and blowers. The engines produced 320 horsepower under full steam, which enabled the ironclad to make 9 knots. Another firm, Clute Brothers Foundry of Schenectady, New York, was contracted to build the special anchor hoisting mechanism, engine room grates, gun carriages, and the auxiliary steam engines.

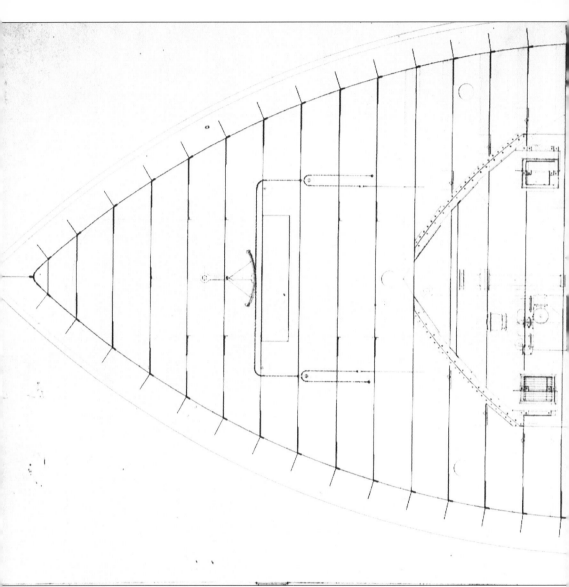

Several features of Ericsson's original design were discarded or modified due to time constraints. He proposed to arm the ironclad with his own steam gun and proto-torpedoes (also called "hydrostatic javelins"), but these weapons were replaced by a conventional pair of Dahlgren smoothbores in the turret. Ericsson had planned a sloping deck. Instead, a simpler flat deck was constructed. The turret was originally conceived as a hemispheric turret. It, too, was replaced with a less complex cylindrical turret. The turret was a massive structure, over 9 feet high and 20 feet in diameter. The walls were constructed of eight layers of 1-inch plate bolted together with overlapping joints. An additional layer was added to the turret's interior to protect the gun

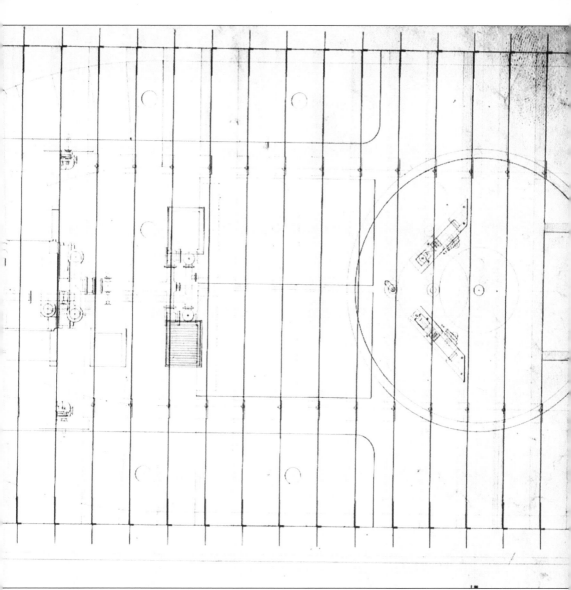

crew from flying bolts caused by cannon fire.

The Abbott firm had made special curved plates, which were shipped from Baltimore to New York and then fitted onto the turret's frame by Novelty Iron Works. The turret, weighing 120 tons, was far too heavy to transport intact to Greenpoint. Novelty disassembled it and sections were reassembled on the ironclad's deck at Continental Iron Works. The turret was placed into a large brass ring set into the deck and would turn on huge ball bearings, each 10 inches in diameter. A small steam engine connected to a central, vertical drive shaft by four large horizontal gears, placed the turret in motion. The entire system was operated by one man.

By January 1862, the ironclad was beginning to take shape, and Gideon Welles named Lieutenant John Lorimer Worden to assume command of the novel vessel. Worden, a native of New York, had served in the U.S. Navy since 1834 and had been a prisoner of war after a secret mission to Fort Pickens in Pensacola Bay, Florida. Recently exchanged, Worden was advised by Commodore Joseph Smith of the Ironclad Board, "This vessel is an experiment." Worden visited the ironclad and accepted the command. On the very same day, he advised Smith, "After a hasty examination of her," he was, "induced to believe that she may prove a success. At all events, I am quite willing to be an agent in testing her capabilities."

The ironclad also needed a name. Assistant Secretary of the Navy Gustavus Vasa Fox asked Ericsson for a suggestion, to which he replied the following:

> In accordance with your request, I now submit for your approbation a name for the floating battery at Greenpoint. The impregnable and aggressive nature of this structure will admonish the leaders of the Southern Rebellion that the batteries on the banks of their rivers will no longer present barriers to the entrance of the Union forces.
>
> The iron-clad intruder will thus prove a severe monitor to those leaders. But there are other leaders who will also be startled and admonished by the booming of the guns from the impregnable iron turret. "Downing Street" will hardly view with indifference this last "Yankee notion," this monitor. To the Lord of the Admiralty the new craft will be a monitor . . . On these and many similar grounds I propose to name the new battery *Monitor*.

Fox could only agree with Ericsson's logic.

The *Monitor* was launched on January 30, 1862, and there were many skeptics present. One observer told Acting Master Louis N. Stodder that "You had better take a good look at her now as you won't see her after she strikes water. She's bound to go to the bottom of the East River and stick there, sure." Instead of sinking, the *Monitor* slid down the ways with a defiant Ericsson standing on the deck. The Union command was elated and ready for the ironclad to see service. Fox wrote Ericsson, "I congratulate you and trust she will be a success. Hurry her for sea, as the *Merrimack* is nearly ready at Norfolk and we wish to send her there." Gideon Welles had hoped to get the *Monitor* to Hampton Roads while the Confederate ironclad was still under construction. Welles believed that the *Monitor* could easily steam up the Elizabeth River past the Confederate batteries and destroy the *Merrimack* as it sat in drydock.

Ericsson had hoped to mount two 15-inch Dahlgrens in the turret, but Worden could only locate two 11-inch versions, which were removed from the decommissioned six-gun steam sloop U.S.S. *Dacotah*. A 15-pound charge of powder would enable these Dahlgrens to hurl a 166-pound solid shot or a 136-pound explosive shell up to 1,700 yards. Each 11-inch Dahlgren weighed over 8 tons, and their massive size left little room in the turret for the gun crews. The turret was fitted with huge pendulum port shutters to protect the turret's interior when the guns were being reloaded. In fact, a special loop-hole was bored into each shutter to allow the cannon to be sponged, wormed, and reloaded when the shutter was closed. A port shutter design error allowed only one gun to fire at a time, thus reducing the *Monitor*'s broadside in half. A modification was made to correct this problem, but the port stoppers remained difficult to operate.

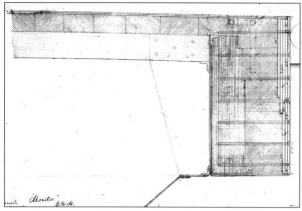

The *Monitor* was delivered to the U.S. Navy for testing on February 19, 1862. Overall, the *Monitor* was 173 feet in length, weighed 776 tons, and had a beam of 41.5 feet. The ironclad's draft was 11 feet with a freeboard of less than 1 foot. It was virtually awash with the sea. The hull was sheathed with 1 inch of iron, and the deck was covered with 4.5 inches of armor plate. All of the ship's machinery, magazine, and quarters were positioned below the waterline to protect these vital parts from cannon fire. The officer's quarters were small and well appointed. Ericsson installed curtains even though there were no ports; the quarters were below sea level. The inventor had allowed for hammock space for only half the crew. He rationalized that the other half would always be on duty. Because the ship was partially submerged, Ericsson even created a unique waste disposal system. A pilothouse and the turret were the only features protruding from the deck. The pilothouse was a rectangular box of iron, standing 3 feet above the deck and made of nine 9-by-12-inch bars bolted at the corners. A .5-inch observation slit was included below the upper tier of iron bars. The anchor well was located forward of the pilothouse, enabling crewmen to raise and lower the anchor from within the ironclad. The *Monitor* featured over 40 of Ericsson's patented inventions.

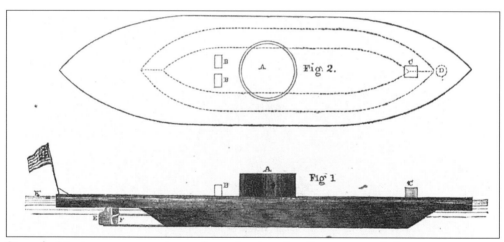

Since the *Monitor* was an experimental vessel and was hastily constructed, there were numerous problems and defects. The communication link (a speaking tube) between the pilothouse and turret only worked when the turret faced toward the pilothouse. This circumstance would certainly delay communications during combat as well as place the pilothouse at possible risk from an errant broadside.

Of even greater concern were two problems discovered during the ironclad's initial trials. The *Monitor* could only make 3.5 knots instead of the planned 9 knots. This speed problem was eventually corrected with an engine valve adjustment. On February 27, the ironclad steamed into the East River, but the steering became extremely erratic. "We ran first to the New York side then to the Brooklyn and so back and forth across the river, first to one side then to the other, like a drunken man on a sidewalk," wrote one of the ironclad's officers. Eventually the *Monitor* crashed into a dock and had to be towed back to the Brooklyn Navy Yard.

Hiram Paulding, commandant of the Brooklyn Navy Yard, suggested that the *Monitor* be placed back into drydock to correct the steering problem with a new rudder. Ericsson flatly refused declaring, "Put in a new rudder. The *Monitor* is mine, and I say it shall not be done. They would waste a month in doing it. I will make her steer easily in three days." The rudder was seriously overbalanced and Ericsson, assisted by Chief Engineer Alban C. Stimers (pictured here), corrected the problem by installing a series of pulleys between the tiller and the steering wheel drum. Stimers, who had been assigned to the *Monitor* project by the U.S. Navy to supervise the ironclad's construction, worked very well with Ericsson. The brilliant 34-year-old engineer was assigned to stay with the *Monitor* to judge its effectiveness in action.

The *Monitor* was commissioned on February 25, 1862, as a fourth-rate ship. Captain John A. Dahlgren called the vessel as she lay moored at Brooklyn Navy Yard, "a mere speck, like a hat on the surface." Commander David Dixon Porter, who had been assigned the task of assessing the ironclad's combat capabilities, declared the *Monitor* "a perfect success, and capable of defeating anything that then floated." Lieutenant Worden, meanwhile, prepared the ironclad for sea. Worden assembled a hand-picked volunteer crew, which eventually numbered 16 officers and 49 men. Most were amazed by the ironclad as Acting Assistant Paymaster William F. Keeler wrote to his wife, "I shall not attempt a description of it now, but you may rest assured your better half will be in no more danger from rebel complements than if he was seated with you at home. There isn't danger enough to give us any glory."

Others were uncertain of the *Monitor*'s abilities. Master Louis N. Stodder (pictured here) noted that "she was rather a hasty job, was the *Monitor*." Quartermaster Peter Truscott added, "She was a little bit the strangest craft I had ever seen." Seaman David R. Ellis made perhaps the most telling remark about the ironclad as it readied to leave New York commenting, "She had not been pronounced seaworthy, and no one could safely judge of her fighting qualities." Nevertheless, Commodore Hiram Paulding ordered Worden, "When the weather permits you will proceed with the *Monitor* under your command to Hampton Roads and on your arrival report to the senior officer there . . . wishing you a safe passage." On March 5, 1862, the *Monitor* was ready to leave New York; however, another steering malfunction delayed departure.

On the afternoon of March 6, 1862, the U.S.S. *Monitor* left New York under tow by the steam tug *Seth Low* (pictured here), accompanied by the steamers *Sachem* and *Camtuck*. The weather was fine when the ironclad began its voyage. By the next morning, a gale had worked up the coast and, as Alban Stimers noted, "the sea commenced to wash right across the deck." Even though Ericsson had designed the turret to form a water-tight seal fitting into the brass ring on the deck, Navy officials insisted on jacking the turret up on wedges and caulking it with hemp. This modification failed to stop water entering the ironclad. The water gushed through the turret "like a waterfall." Executive Officer Lieutenant Samuel Dana Greene wrote that the angry sea "would strike the pilot-house and go over the turret in beautiful curves, and it came through the narrow eye-holes in the pilot-house with such force as to knock the helmsman completely around from the wheel." Paymaster Keeler noted that by morning of March 7, "the top of every sea that breaks against our side rolls unobstructed over the deck dashing and foaming at a terrible rate."

Ericsson had fitted a temporary 6-foot funnel over the existing deck-flush smokestack to protect against high seas. Nevertheless, water soon began to come down the smokestack and wet the belts, which operated blowers circulating air throughout the vessel. Without air, the coal fires were extinguished, and fumes overcame the engineers and firemen. They were saved from suffocation only by being taken to the top of the turret. The boiler fires went out, and the engines ceased, stopping the steam-powered large-capacity Worthington and Adams pumps. Greene later wrote that "the water continued to pour through the hawse-hole, and over and down the smoke-stacks and blower-pipes, in such quantities that there was imminent danger that the ship would founder." Since Worden was seasick, Greene set about saving the ship. It was rapidly filling with water. Hand pumps were tried, but they were not powerful enough to pull the water out through the turret hatch. Greene organized a bucket line to bail out the water; unfortunately, it did little to combat the rising water. Acting Assistant Paymaster Keeler wrote later about the foundering vessel, "things for a time looked pretty blue, as though we might have to give up the ship." The *Monitor*'s flag was flying upside down indicating distress, but only when Greene hailed and ordered the *Seth Low* to tow the *Monitor* toward calmer waters was the ironclad saved.

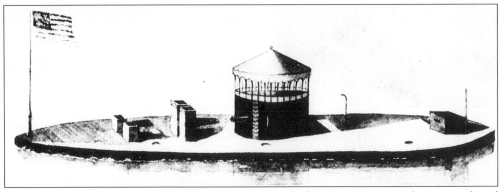

Stimers was now able to restart the engines and work the steam pumps. The storm abated during the evening. Greene had just laid down in his bunk at around 3 a.m. on March 8, when he wrote the following:

> I was startled by the most infernal noise I ever heard in my life . . . We were just passing a shoal and the sea suddenly became very rough . . . It came up with tremendous force through our anchor well and forced air through our hawse-pipe where the chain comes, and there the water would come through in a perfect stream, clear to our berth deck, over the ward-room table.

The waves were once again crashing over the *Monitor*'s decks, and there was danger that the blower system would once again fail.

Lieutenant Greene (pictured here) "began to think that the *Monitor* would never see daylight" as the wheel ropes jumped off the steering wheel and the ship began to sheer, stressing its towline with the *Seth Low*. Fortunately, the steering problem was fixed and the ironclad was able to ride out the storm until daylight. The crew of the *Seth Low* noticed the *Monitor*'s distress and towed her near the shore. The *Monitor* had survived two close encounters with the angry sea and by late afternoon on March 8, 1862, neared the Chesapeake Capes. Samuel Dana Greene, a Maryland native and Annapolis graduate, wrote later about the stormy trip from New York, "I think I lived 10 good years."

Four

SINK BEFORE
YOU SURRENDER

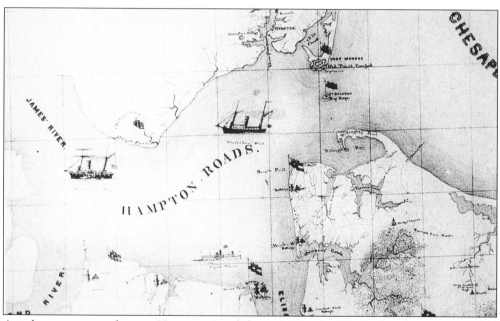

A stalemate remained across Hampton Roads by early March 1862. Both navies were rushing their ironclads toward completion to attain naval superiority in Hampton Roads. Control of this major harbor was deemed critical. The Confederates needed to defend the James River approach to Richmond as well as Norfolk's industrial center. The Federals, in turn, had already proven the harbor's immense value for launching expeditions against the Southern coast. More importantly, U.S. Army General-in-Chief George Brinton McClellan had also presented his ambitious plan in March to "take Fort Monroe as a base, and operate with complete security . . . up the Peninsula" and capture the Confederate capital at Richmond. The entire Army of the Potomac now planned to use Hampton Roads, and the campaign's success hinged upon the U.S. Navy's control of the harbor and ability to move with the Army up the James River. Lincoln was concerned about the campaign's feasibility, but was assured by Assistant Navy Secretary Gustavus Fox that "you need not give yourself any trouble about that vessel."

Flag Officer Louis Malesherbes Goldsborough had replaced Commodore Silas Horton Stringham as commander of the North Atlantic Blockading Squadron in September 1861. Goldsborough was born in Washington, D.C. and entered the U.S. Navy as a midshipman at the age of seven. A veteran of the Seminole and Mexican Wars and a former superintendent of the U.S. Naval Academy in Annapolis, Goldsborough was a huge (reports indicate that he weighed well over 300 pounds) and intimidating man with a powerful temper. One naval officer noted that Goldsborough possessed "manners so rough, so that he would almost frighten a subordinate out of his wits." Since assuming command of the squadron, Goldsborough continuously bombarded Gideon Welles with reports about the Confederate ironclad. On October 17, 1861, Goldsborough wrote Welles noting, "I have received further minute reliable information with regard to the preparation of the *Merrimack* for an attack on Newport News and these roads, and I am quite satisfied that unless her stability be compromised by her heavy top works of wood and iron and her weight of batteries, she will in all probability, prove to be exceedingly formidable."

To counter any possible threat from the Confederate ironclad, Goldsborough turned the Hampton Roads blockading force into a strong complement of warships. At the fleet's heart were the two sister steam screw frigates U.S.S. *Minnesota* and U.S.S. *Roanoke*. Each carried an impressive broadside. The *Minnesota*'s battery consisted of one 10-inch and twenty-eight 9-inch Dahlgren smoothbores, fourteen 8-inch guns, two 24-pounders, and two 12-pounders. She was Goldsborough's flagship. The station also included three sailing warships: the 50-gun U.S.S. *Congress*, the 44-gun U.S.S. *St. Lawrence*, and the 24-gun sloop-of-war U.S.S. *Cumberland*. The *Cumberland* featured perhaps the most powerful armament in Goldsborough's Hampton Roads station. Formerly a 44-gun sailing frigate and flagship of the Mediterranean and African squadrons, in 1856, the *Cumberland* had been "razed" down to a sloop and armed with twenty-two 9-inch Dahlgren smoothbores, one 10-inch Dahlgren smoothbore, and a powerful 70-pounder rifle. The squadron was supported by the steamer *Cambridge*, the store ship *Brandywine*, three coal ships, a hospital ship, five tugboats, a side-wheel steamer, and a sailing bark. Goldsborough, before leaving for North Carolina with Burnside's expedition to capture Roanoke Island, had planned to confront the Confederate ironclad when it entered Hampton Roads by bringing all of the vessels in a crossfire.

"Nothing, I think," wrote Goldsborough, "but very close work can be of service in accomplishing the destruction of the *Merrimack* and even of that a great deal may be necessary." There were concerns, however, that the Union ships without the support of an ironclad of their own, might be unable to confront the Confederate ironclad. Lieutenant Joseph Smith of the *Congress* noted that his frigate "had been a model in her day." Nevertheless, he was worried that since all of his cannon were older smoothbores, "we should only be a good target for them, as none of our guns could throw a shot to them." There were shortages of veteran seamen and several ships, especially the *Roanoke*, that required major repairs. The *Roanoke*'s engines were useless, and Captain John Marston, the ship's commander and acting commander of the Hampton Roads station, lamented that his ship as well as the others in Hampton Roads could not be overhauled "as long as the *Merrimack* is held as a rod over us."

The Union fleet was expecting the Confederate ironclad, as Captain Marston noted, "I am anxiously expecting her and believe I am ready." Rumors of the Confederate ironclad's sortie into Hampton Roads were announced daily. Marston wrote Gideon Welles on February 21, 1862, that "By a dispatch which I received late last evening from General Wool, I learn that the *Merrimack* will positively attack Newport News within five days, acting in conjunction with the *Jamestown* and *Yorktown* from the James River, and the attack will be at night." Union intelligence was very close to the truth about Confederate plans. Nevertheless, the Confederate ironclad still did not appear as reported.

Captain Gershom Jaques Van Brunt (pictured here), commander of the U.S.S. *Minnesota*, wrote Goldsborough, "We have nothing new here; all is quiet. The *Merrimack* is still invisible to us, but report says she is ready to come out. I sincerely wish she would; I am quite tired of hearing of her." Van Brunt added that "the sooner she gives us the opportunity to test her strength the better."

Major General John Ellis Wool from his headquarters at Fort Monroe added to the litany of reports and concerns about the impending strike of the Confederate ironclad. Wool believed that his position at Camp Butler on Newport News Point would be threatened by an attack by the *Merrimack*. Goldsborough, who considered Wool to be an "inflated fool," stationed the U.S.S. *Congress* and U.S.S. *Cumberland* off Newport News Point to provide naval support to Camp Butler and to seal off elements of the Confederate James River Squadron from entering Hampton Roads in support of the *Merrimack*. The tugboats *Dragon* and *Zouave* were assigned to support these sailing ships in case they needed to be quickly moved to respond to any attack by the Confederate ironclad. Both ships were on alert awaiting the *Virginia* in early March. Lieutenant Thomas O. Selfridge of the *Congress* noted in his memoirs that reports of her expected appearance came so often, it became a standing joke with the ship's company.

56

Mallory's orders for prompt action had not been lost on Franklin Buchanan. Buchanan sought to make the most of the tactical superiority that his ironclad would give the Confederacy by coordinating a joint attack against the Federal forces at Newport News Point with Major General John Bankhead Magruder's Army of the Peninsula. Buchanan envisioned such an attack dislodging the Union hold on Hampton Roads. He addressed Magruder, known as "Prince John," on March 2, 1862, "It is my intention to be off Newport News early on Friday morning next unless some accident occurs to the *Virginia* to prevent it, this I do not anticipate. You may therefore look out for me at the time named. My plan is to destroy the Frigates first, if possible, and then turn my attention to the battery on shore. I sincerely hope that acting together we may be successful in destroying many of the enemy." Even though Prince John had initially agreed to this plan, he backed off as time neared, stating that "the roads were too impassable for artillery" and lamenting that the Federals had been reinforced. Magruder also advised the Confederate command in Richmond that "no one ship can produce such an impression upon the troops at Newport News Point as to cause them to evacuate the fort." The Confederate general believed that "no important advantages can be obtained by the *Merrimac* further than to demonstrate her power, which as she is liable to be injured by a chance shot at this critical time, which had better be reserved to defeat the enemy's serious efforts against Norfolk and James River."

Buchanan (seen here on the right) was undaunted by Magruder's refusal to participate in his attack against Newport News Point and ignored his suggestion that the *Virginia* be used as a floating battery in the James River to protect the Confederate Army's right flank. "Old Buck" had been assigned to the *Virginia* because of his aggressive nature, and he intended to take his ironclad into action as quickly as possible. He planned to take the *Virginia* down the Elizabeth River during the evening of March 6 to surprise the Federals with an early morning attack on March 7. A severe gale (the same one that almost sank the *Monitor*) delayed the scheduled foray. The *Virginia* required calm waters to safely operate, and the pilots refused to guide the deep draught ironclad through the Elizabeth River's narrow channel at night. Even though the *Virginia* was still considered "by no means ready for service," Buchanan was determined to take the ironclad into action on the next day.

On March 8, 1862, the weather cleared, and Buchanan prepared his ironclad for action. The casemate was coated with a thick coating of tallow, as Catesby Jones noted that it would "increase the tendency of the projectiles to glance." Buchanan hoisted his red flag officer ensign and ordered the workmen, who were still laboring on the *Virginia*'s armor, off the vessel. At 11 a.m., the *Virginia* cast off from the dock and began its trip down the Elizabeth River. Buchanan's aggressive intentions took most of the crew by surprise, as he had only told one or two of his officers that he intended to attack the Union fleet that day. Lieutenant John R. Eggleston remembered that the crew thought "we were going on an ordinary trial trip." Buchanan, however, was focused on the enemy vessels. Just before leaving the dock, he asked Chief Engineer G. Ashton Ramsay, "What would happen to your engines and boilers if there should be a collision?" Ramsay replied that all of the machinery was securely braced and the 10-mile trip down river would be sufficient to test the engines' reliability. Buchanan was satisfied with Ramsay's opinion and declared, "I am going to ram the *Cumberland*. I am told she has the new rifled guns, the only ones in their whole fleet we have cause to fear. The moment we are out in the Roads, I'm going to make right for her and ram her."

As the *Virginia* steamed down the Elizabeth River accompanied by her two gunboat consorts, C.S.S. *Beaufort* and C.S.S. *Raleigh*, both sides of the riverbank were "thronged with people." Ship surgeon Dinwiddie B. Phillips commented, "most of them, perhaps, attracted by our novel appearance, and desirous of witnessing our movements through the water." "Few, if any," Phillips added, "entertained an exalted idea of our efficiency, and many predicted a total failure." Midshipman Hardin B. Littlepage remembered one man shouting, "Go on with your old metallic coffin! She will never amount to anything else!" Others among the spectators realized that this was the day, according to Lieutenant William Harwar Parker of the *Beaufort*, "that here was to be tried the great experiment of the ram and iron-clad in naval warfare." The *Virginia* appeared fearsome to many onlookers, yet there were still problems on board the ironclad. "From the start we saw that she was slow, not over five knots," Lieutenant John Taylor Wood later commented, "She steered so badly that, with her great length it took thirty to forty minutes to turn . . . She was as unmanageable as a water-logged vessel." The huge ironclad's keel was running so close to the river bottom that the ship's rudder could not steer her. The *Virginia* took a towline from the *Beaufort* to help her round a bend in the river.

Buchanan ordered the men to their mid-day meal. A caterer provided the officers with a picnic of "cold tongue and biscuit." When Ashton Ramsay entered the wardroom for his lunch, he noticed Assistant Surgeon Algernon S. Garnett laying out his surgical instruments in preparation for the coming battle. "The sight," Ramsay reflected, "took away my appetite." Buchanan, however, was ready for battle, and once the ironclad neared Craney Island, he stepped onto the gun deck and reportedly informed the crew the following:

> Sailors in a few minutes you will have the long awaited opportunity to show your devotion to your country and our cause. Remember that you are about to strike for your country and your homes, your wives, and your children. The Confederacy expects every man to do his duty, beat to quarters!

Buchanan reminded everyone that the "whole world is watching you today." He sent a message to the commanders of his escort gunboats that if the battle turned against them, he would hoist the signal "Sink before you Surrender."

By 1:30 p.m., the *Virginia* dropped its towline from the *Beaufort* and entered Hampton Roads at high tide. The crew could see the entire Federal fleet before them arrayed in a line that stretched from Newport News Point to Fort Monroe. Two French warships, the *Gassendi* and *Catinat*, were in the harbor awaiting the events which were soon to unfold. Nevertheless, the Confederates appeared to have achieved a tactical surprise, as clothing hung from the rigging of Union ships. "Nothing indicated," John Taylor Wood wrote, "that we were expected." Buchanan now turned the *Virginia* into the channel toward his targets at Newport News Point. This caused some reflection among several Confederate officers, who had previously served on the *Congress* and the *Cumberland*. Lieutenant John Eggleston fondly remembered his time spent aboard the *Congress*, "little did I think then that I should ever lift a hand for her destruction."

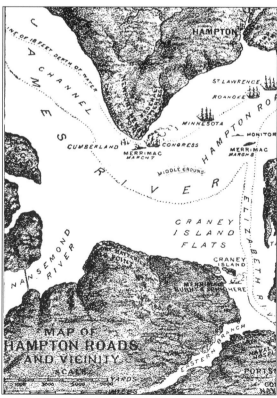

March 8 "was a fine mild day, such as is common in southern Virginia during early Spring," one Union officer wrote. The peaceful scene was broken when the Confederate vessels were observed steaming out of the Elizabeth River around 12:45 p.m. One crew member of the *Congress* supposedly announced to the deck officer, "I wish you would take a glass and have a look over there, Sir. I believe that thing is a-comin' down at last." Another Union sailor remembered that day and his first sight of the *Virginia*, "Pretty soon that great black thing, different from any vessel ever seen before, poked her nose around Sewell's Point." The Union tug, *Zouave*, steamed from Newport News toward Pig Point to investigate. "It did not take us long to find out," noted Acting Master Henry Reaney of the *Zouave*, that it was the long-awaited Confederate ironclad. "We had not gone over two miles," Reaney continued, "when we saw what to all appearances looked like the roof of a very big barn belching forth smoke as from a chimney on fire." The *Zouave* fired several shells from its 30-pounder Parrott at the huge ironclad and returned to the Newport News anchorage. The photograph on the left is of Joseph Fairchild Baker, commander of the U.S.S. *Congress* Marine Guard.

"Suddenly, huge volumes of smoke began to pour from the funnels of the frigates *Minnesota* and *Roanoke* at Old Point," Ashton Ramsay recalled. "They had seen us and were getting up steam. Bright colored signal flags were run up and down the masts of all the ships of the Federal Fleet," Ramsay continued. "The *Congress* shook out her topsails, down came the clothes-lines on the *Cumberland* and boats were lowered and dropped astern." "Men jumped lively," one Union sailor recalled as the Federal fleet prepared for action. Brigadier General Joseph K.F. Mansfield, commander of Camp Butler, telegraphed Major General John E. Wool at Fort Monroe alerting him that "The *Merrimack* is being towed down by two steamers past Cranby [sic] Island towards Sewell's Point." Shortly thereafter he reported again, "The *Merrimack* is close at hand." As the crews and officers of the *Congress* and *Cumberland* readied themselves for combat, other vessels in the Federal fleet struggled to reach Newport News Point. The *Roanoke*, her engines disabled, was taken under tow and the *Minnesota* got underway. Both ships were too late to save the two sailing ships. Pictured here on the right is Captain Charles Heywood, commander of the U.S.S. *Cumberland*'s Marine Guard.

It took the *Virginia* over an hour to steam across Hampton Roads. Once within range, the Union ships and shore batteries began shelling the ironclad. The Federal shot and shell harmlessly bounced off the *Virginia*. The shot "had no effect on her," as Thomas O. Selfridge (inset picture) recounted, "but glanced off like pebble stones." At 2:20 p.m., the Confederates opened fire at the Union ships. The *Beaufort*, flying her pennant from the Battle of Roanoke Island, fired the first Confederate shot from her 32-pounder bow rifle at the *Congress*. Buchanan, however, waited until the range was less than 1,500 yards. Then he ordered Lieutenant Charles C. Simms to fire the 7-inch Brooke bow rifle at the *Cumberland*. The *Virginia*'s first shot hit the *Cumberland* at the starboard rail, showering splinters across the deck. The second shell decimated an entire gun crew and disabled the gun itself. Dead and wounded were everywhere. "No one flinched," Selfridge recalled, "but went on loading and firing, taking the place of some comrade, killed or wounded, as they had been told to do." One Northern correspondent wrote that he saw "from the ship's scuppers running streams of crimson gore."

The *Virginia* had now come abreast of the *Congress*. When the Confederate ironclad passed the hapless frigate, she unleashed her starboard broadside at the *Congress*. The effect was devastating. One shell went though a gunport, dismounting the gun and "sweeping the men about it back into a heap, bruised and bleeding." Hot shot from the *Virginia* rumbled through the frigate starting two fires, one of which threatened to ignite the *Congress*'s powder magazine. The *Congress* appeared critically damaged; however, nothing would delay Buchanan's intended rendezvous with the U.S.S. *Cumberland*. The *Virginia* continued toward the sloop "like some devilish and superhuman monster, or the horrid creation of a nightmare." The *Cumberland* kept up its fire against the oncoming ironclad, but her shot "struck and glanced off, having no more effect than peas from a pop-gun." "At her prow I could see the iron ram projecting," the *Cumberland*'s pilot A.B. Smith remembered, "straight forward, somewhat above the water's edge, and apparently a mass of iron." Smith sadly reflected that "it was impossible for our vessel to get out of her way."

"Like a huge half-submerged crocodile," the *Virginia* broke through the anti-torpedo obstructions surrounding the *Cumberland* and rammed the sloop on the starboard side of her bow. Lieutenant Jones recalled that "the noise was heard above the din of battle." The 1,500-pound cast-iron ram punched a hole into the *Cumberland*'s berth deck. According to Lieutenant John Taylor Wood, it was "wide enough to drive in a horse and cart." The *Cumberland* was mortally wounded, the ramming made only worse by a simultaneous shot from

the *Virginia*'s bow rifle, which killed ten men. "We've sank the *Cumberland*," Lieutenant Robert Minor shouted running down the gundeck waving his cap. Minor would later write, "The crash into the *Cumberland* was terrific in its results. Our cleaver fairly opened her side." Tons of water were now gushing into the *Cumberland*, and she began to sink very rapidly to starboard; thus, trapping the *Virginia*'s ram within her.

"Soon, however, I heard the reports of our own guns and then there came a tremor throughout the whole ship," wrote Assistant Engineer E.A. Jack, "and I was never thrown from the coal bucket upon which I was sitting. This is when we drove into the *Cumberland* with our own ram. Then, the cracking and breaking of her timbers told full well how fatal to her that collision was. Then, there was a settling motion of our vessel that aroused suspicion that our ship had been injured too, and was sinking . . ." Just before ramming the *Cumberland*, Buchanan ordered the ironclad's engines to be reversed. The *Virginia* was caught by the weight of the sinking *Cumberland* as its engines labored. Chief Engineer Ashton Ramsay wrote, "the vessel was shaken in every fiber." Ramsay then, as the *Virginia*'s bow began to depress into the water, heard an explosion in the engine room. He thought the boilers had burst, struggling to back the *Virginia* away from the *Cumberland*. Instead, it was only an enemy shell exploding in the funnel. The crisis was quickly over, as the current turned the ironclad alongside the *Cumberland*. The ram, which was faultily mounted, broke off and the *Virginia* was freed. "Like a wasp we could sting but once," wrote Ramsay, "leaving the sting in the wound."

Lieutenant Thomas O. Selfridge later lamented that he failed to seize the initiative to drop the sloop's starboard anchor down onto the *Virginia*'s deck as the ironclad stood alongside the *Cumberland*. Selfridge believed the anchor could have acted as a grappling hook and pulled the ironclad under the James River as the *Cumberland* sank. This moment of opportunity, limited by the mounting casualties, quickly slipped away from the Union officer. The *Virginia*'s engines finally reversed, and the ironclad was freed from the sinking sloop.

Buchanan now positioned the ironclad parallel to the *Cumberland*, and for the next half hour they exchanged cannon fire. Both ships were engulfed in smoke as the *Cumberland* sent "solid broadsides in quick succession . . . into the *Merrimac* at a distance of not more than one hundred yards." Selfridge was "fighting mad when I saw the shells from my guns were producing no effect upon the iron sides of the *Merrimac*." Unbeknownst to the *Cumberland*'s crew, the sloop inflicted serious damage to the *Virginia* during this phase of the battle. The ironclad's smokestack was riddled. The damaged funnel caused the gundeck to be filled with smoke, "making it so dense we could hardly breathe." The stack's condition lessened the draft of the ironclad's boilers and caused the *Virginia* to lower her speed. One shot cut the ironclad's anchor chain, which whipped inboard, killing two men and wounding five others. The *Cumberland*'s three broadsides swept away the *Virginia*'s starboard cutter, howitzers, stanchions, and iron railings.

The *Cumberland*'s gunners aimed at the *Virginia*'s gunports, hoping to send a solid shot inside the casemate. A gunner was cut in half by a shot from the *Cumberland* while swabbing the forward Brooke rifle. Two of the *Virginia*'s broadside guns were disabled when their muzzles were shot off. Despite the effective broadsides from the *Cumberland*, the ironclad kept up its punishing cannonade against the sloop. "On our gundeck the men were fighting like demons," Ashton Ramsay recalled. "There was no thought or time for the wounded and dying as they tugged away at their guns, training, and sighting their pieces while the orders rang out: 'Sponge, load, fire.'" Ramsay observed the officers shouting to the gun crews; "Keep away from the side ports, don't lean against the shield, look out for sharpshooters," rang the warnings. "Some of our men who failed to heed them and leaned back against the shield were stunned and carried below, bleeding at the ears."

The *Virginia*'s sloped sides, coated with grease to help deflect shot, began to crackle and pop from the heat. Midshipman Hardin B. Littlepage wrote that the ironclad seemed to be "frying from one end to the other." Littlepage later recounted one exciting exchange between crew members Jack Cronin and John Hunt: " 'Jack, don't this smell like hell?' 'It certainly does, and I think that we'll all be there in a few minutes.' "

It was indeed hell on the *Cumberland*. Master Moses S. Stuyvesant remembered it as "a scene of carnage and destruction never to be recalled without horror." "The shot and shell from the *Merrimack* crashed through the wooden sides of the *Cumberland* as if they had been made of paper," remembered Acting Master's Mate Charles O'Neil, "carrying huge splinters with them and dealing death and destruction on every hand." O'Neil was spattered with "the blood and brains" of Master's Mate John M. Harrington when a shell whizzed pass, and he remembered how the *Cumberland*'s "once clean and beautiful deck was slippery with blood, blackened with powder and looked like a slaughterhouse."

Lieutenant George Upham Morris, the *Cumberland*'s executive officer and acting commander, strove to save the Union vessel. Morris (pictured here) attempted to turn the *Cumberland* on her anchor cable to either bring more guns into action against the ironclad or cut the cable in an effort to save the ship by running her aground. It was too late, as water had already reached the *Cumberland*'s berth deck and the ship was clearly doomed. About 3:35 p.m., Morris gave the order to abandon ship, exhorting the remaining crew members to "Give them a Broadside boys, as She goes." The *Cumberland* then lurched forward with a roar and sank in just over 50 feet of water. "She went down bravely, with her colors flying," Catesby Jones remembered. The *Cumberland*'s masts protruded above the waves, the flag marking the spot where 121 Union sailors had gallantly perished.

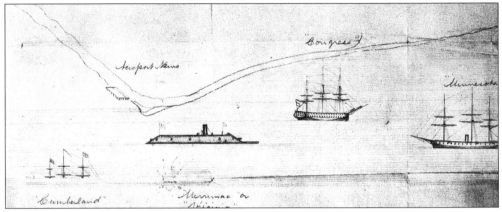

Having destroyed the *Cumberland*, Buchanan now turned his ironclad toward the U.S.S. *Congress*. The *Virginia*, because of its draft and poor steering, was forced to go up the James River to complete its turn. This maneuver took over 30 minutes and was only accomplished with the assistance of the *Raleigh* and *Beaufort*. Meanwhile, the *Congress*, which was already seriously damaged, endeavored to escape the ironclad. The *Zouave* helped to run the *Congress* onto the shoal under the supposed protection of the Federal shore batteries. The *Congress* was unfortunately unable to position herself parallel to shore so that her broadside could help protect the frigate from the approaching *Virginia*. Instead, the *Congress* ran aground with her bow facing Newport News Point; thus, leaving just her stern guns available to return fire. The three other Union capital ships in Hampton Roads, U.S.S. *Minnesota*, U.S.S. *Roanoke*, and U.S.S. *St. Lawrence*, had all run aground rushing to the aid of the Federal forces at Newport News Point. The *St. Lawrence* and *Roanoke* were freed from the shoals, but seeing that wooden ships were powerless to stop the rampaging Confederate ironclad, they retreated towards Old Point Comfort and the protection of Fort Monroe. The *Minnesota*, however, remained aground on the Middle Ground shoal 1.5 miles from the *Congress*.

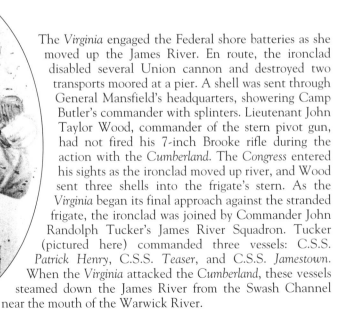

The *Virginia* engaged the Federal shore batteries as she moved up the James River. En route, the ironclad disabled several Union cannon and destroyed two transports moored at a pier. A shell was sent through General Mansfield's headquarters, showering Camp Butler's commander with splinters. Lieutenant John Taylor Wood, commander of the stern pivot gun, had not fired his 7-inch Brooke rifle during the action with the *Cumberland*. The *Congress* entered his sights as the ironclad moved up river, and Wood sent three shells into the frigate's stern. As the *Virginia* began its final approach against the stranded frigate, the ironclad was joined by Commander John Randolph Tucker's James River Squadron. Tucker (pictured here) commanded three vessels: C.S.S. *Patrick Henry*, C.S.S. *Teaser*, and C.S.S. *Jamestown*. When the *Virginia* attacked the *Cumberland*, these vessels steamed down the James River from the Swash Channel near the mouth of the Warwick River.

Tucker took his small squadron past the Union batteries. The *Teaser* and *Jamestown* escaped without damage; however, the *Patrick Henry* received a shot through her steam drum. The *Patrick Henry* (pictured here), formerly the steamer *Yorktown*, was armed with ten guns and featured an iron shield to protect her engines. She was the most powerful Confederate ship in Virginia waters until the emergence of the C.S.S. *Virginia*. While the *Patrick Henry* received emergency repairs, the *Teaser* and *Jamestown* joined the *Virginia* and her escorts in the final attack on the *Congress*. The *Raleigh* and *Beaufort* were already shelling the *Congress* while the *Virginia* completed its turn. The *Raleigh*, however, was put out of action by a disabled gun (its only fire power), and the *Beaufort*'s fire had little impact on the frigate.

Just before 4 p.m., the *Virginia* steamed within 200 yards of the *Congress* and began shelling the grounded frigate. The *Congress*'s stern was quickly demolished and the main deck was "literally reeking with slaughter." Blood from the frigate's deck, wrote Henry Reaney of the *Zouave*, poured "onto our deck like water on wash-deck morning." The *Zouave* was hit by several shells from the ironclad, which destroyed the tug's figurehead and pilothouse. Reaney, once he realized that nothing could be done to save the *Congress*, cut the line to the doomed frigate and steamed toward the *Minnesota*. A shell hit the *Zouave*'s rudderpost, virtually disabling the vessel. The tug fled the scene.

Lieutenant Joseph B. Smith, acting commander of the *Congress*, struggled to keep his ship in action. Several large fires were raging throughout the ship, and over a quarter of the crew were killed or wounded. About 4:20 p.m., Smith (pictured here) was struck by a shell fragment, which tore off his head and a portion of his shoulder. The ship's command now rested on the shoulders of Lieutenant Austin Pendergrast. Pendergrast, in consultation with the ship's former captain, Commander William Smith, agreed that the *Congress* was helpless and surrender was the only reasonable alternative.

The Confederates were jubilant when they saw the white flag rise above the *Congress*, and Buchanan immediately commanded his gun crews to cease fire. He then ordered the *Raleigh* and *Beaufort* to go alongside the frigate to "take the officers and wounded men prisoners, to permit the others to escape to shore, and to burn the ship." Lieutenant William H. Parker (pictured here in the inset), the *Beaufort*'s commander, went on board the stricken vessel to accept its surrender and commented, "My God, this is terrible. I wish this war was over." Parker accepted the frigate's surrender from Austin Pendergrast and William Smith, but demanded that they also surrender their personal sidearms. As the two Union officers went to retrieve their weapons, Parker ordered the *Jamestown* to the other side of the *Congress* to speed the evacuation of wounded sailors. "I had scarcely given him the order," Parker later wrote, "when a tremendous fire was opened on us from the shore." Several Confederate officers were killed, and Parker himself suffered a minor wound.

Brigadier General Joseph K.F. Mansfield (seen here, center), a 40-year Army veteran and West Point graduate, witnessed the entire fight and reported the following to General Wool at Fort Monroe late that afternoon:

> We want powder by the barrel. We want blankets sent up tonight for crews of the *Cumberland* and *Congress*. The *Merrimack* has had it all her own way this side of Signal Point and will probably burn the *Congress* now aground with white flag flying and our sailors are swimming ashore.

Though the *Congress* may have surrendered, Mansfield certainly had not, and he was determined to strike back at the Confederates.

Mansfield, who when questioned about the propriety of firing on the Confederates, reportedly snapped, "I know the d—d ship has surrendered, but we haven't." He ordered detachments from the 20th Indiana and 1st New York Mounted Rifles with three rifled cannon down to the beach to open fire on the Confederate gunboats. One of the cannon was manned by survivors of the *Cumberland* and commanded by Master Moses Stuyvesant. As his men continued to remove the wounded from the *Congress*, Parker shouted, "Make haste, those scoundrels on the shore are firing at me now." The *Beaufort*, suffering more than ten casualties, backed away from the *Congress* with 30 prisoners on board and steamed toward Craney Island.

Buchanan was enraged by the *Beaufort*'s unauthorized retreat. He did not think highly of Lieutenant Parker, stating that Parker lacked "judgment and discretion." Parker had not informed Buchanan of the situation on board the *Congress*, and "Old Buck" was particularly displeased that Parker had not set fire to the frigate. Robert Dabney Minor, the flag lieutenant on the *Virginia*, noticed that Buchanan was in a rage and that "the old gentleman was very anxious to destroy" the *Congress*. Lieutenant Minor (pictured here) volunteered to go in the *Virginia*'s only remaining cutter to complete the frigate's destruction. He set out in the boat, covered by the tug *Teaser*, with eight men at the oars. "I did not think the Yankees on shore would fire at me on my errand to the *Congress*," Minor later wrote, "but when in about two hundred and fifty yards of her they opened fire on me from the shore . . . and the way the balls danced around my little boat and crew was lively beyond all measure."

Minor was knocked down into the boat, shot in the chest, and two of his men were wounded. "I was only down a second or two, and steering my crippled boat for the *Teaser* . . . ." The *Teaser*, commanded by Lieutenant William A. Webb (pictured here), picked up the survivors and returned them to the *Virginia*. Minor recalled, "It had already been reported that they were firing up on me, and the flag officer, seeing it, deliberately backed our dear old craft up close astern of the *Congress* and poured gun after gun, hot shot, and incendiary shells into her."

Admiral Franklin Buchanan
C.S. NAVY.

Franklin Buchanan's battle blood was now boiling. Lieutenant John R. Eggleston heard Buchanan shout, "Destroy that —— ship! She's firing on our white flag!" Buchanan, who was noted for his excitable nature, then recklessly climbed up on top of the *Virginia* to gain a better view of the action. He was so enraged by the events that he called for a rifle and began firing at the troops on the shore. Buchanan did not go unnoticed, as one member of the 1st New York Mounted Rifles remembered that "whenever a man came up on top of the *Merrimack* we shot at him all together." Such an obvious target, Buchanan was shot in the thigh. He was carried below and ordered Catesby Jones to "Plug hot shot into her and don't leave her until she's afire."

73

Jones now assumed command of the *Virginia* and continued firing on the *Congress* until she was blazing from stem to stern. "Dearly did they pay," wrote Eggleston, "for their unparalleled treachery." Yet, there was still more work for the Confederate ironclad to accomplish in Hampton Roads as the sun began to set. It was after 5 p.m. and the tide had receded so that the *Virginia* could not venture out of the channel without risk of grounding. Nevertheless, Jones headed the *Virginia* toward the stranded *Minnesota*. The *Virginia*, accompanied by the *Jamestown* and *Patrick Henry*, moved to within a mile of the Union steam frigate and began shelling the vessel. Jones had hoped to send hot shot into the helpless *Minnesota*, but the broadsides from the *Cumberland* had disabled the only port side hot shot gun. The ironclad would have to turn around to bring her starboard cannon to bear on the *Minnesota*, but time and tide were against such a maneuver. After an hour of long-range bombardment, the *Virginia* steamed back to its moorings near Sewell's Point. It had grown "so dark that we could not see to point the guns with accuracy," reflected Catesby Jones. By 7 p.m., the battle in Hampton Roads was over, but Jones was determined to renew the attack the next morning.

"It was a great victory," recalled Lieutenant Robert Minor. "The IRON and the HEAVY GUNS did the work." In one afternoon, the *Virginia* devastated the Union fleet and achieved tactical control of Hampton Roads. The Union losses were staggering: two transports destroyed, two capital warships sunk, one steam frigate damaged, and over 280 casualties. (The March 8, 1862 battle would remain the worst U.S. Navy defeat until Pearl Harbor.) The grounded *Minnesota* was hard hit by almost a dozen shells. The vessel's main mast was damaged and her wooden sides penetrated by shot. Most of the *Minnesota*'s officers and crew did not care "to look forward to the morrow, as there was but one termination possible as far as we knew then," Thomas Rae reflected. The Union command was stunned by the defeat. President Abraham Lincoln viewed the March 8 events as the greatest Union calamity since Bull Run. Secretary of War Edwin W. Stanton became "almost frantic," according to Gideon Welles's observations, stating that "The *Merrimac* . . . would destroy every vessel in the service, could lay every city on the coast under contribution, could take Fortress Monroe; McClellan's mistaken purpose to advance must be abandoned." Stanton feared, as Welles noted, that the Confederate ironclad would soon "come up the Potomac and disperse Congress, destroy the Capitol and public buildings; or she might go to New York and Boston and destroy those cities . . ." Little did the Northern leaders realize that the *Virginia* was considered by Franklin Buchanan so unseaworthy that it could not leave Hampton Roads.

When the *Virginia* reached its mooring off Sewell's Point at 8 p.m., civilians and soldiers lined the shore to celebrate and learn more about how the ironclad achieved its great victory. Lieutenants John Taylor Wood and Douglas French Forrest immediately caught a train to Richmond and late that evening presented the flag of the *Congress* to President Jefferson Davis. Catesby Jones instead focused on preparing the *Virginia* for the next day's action. Jones inspected the ironclad for damage and discovered a small leak in the bow, but did not notice that the ram was missing. Despite the missing anchors, boats, flagstaffs, railings, and howitzers, most of which were lost during the fight with the *Cumberland*, Jones believed that the *Virginia* was ready once again to venture out against the Federal fleet.

While the Confederates rejoiced over their victory, Flag Officer Buchanan lay depressed and wounded in his cabin, lamenting that "my brother Paymaster Buchanan was on board the *Congress*." Unbeknownst to Franklin Buchanan, Lieutenant Commander McKean Buchanan (pictured here) had somehow survived the battle. The seriously wounded Flag Officer Buchanan and Lieutenant Minor were finally convinced to leave the ironclad. Chief Surgeon Dinwiddie Phillips supervised this task, and as he returned to the *Virginia* he surveyed the ship's damage. He counted 98 indentations in the iron from enemy shot and noted that the smokestack was so riddled that it "would have permitted a flock of crows to fly through without inconvenience."

The glowing *Congress* provided a spectacular conclusion to the events of March 8. Ashton Ramsay remembered as follows:

All the evening we stood on deck watching the brilliant display of the burning ship. Every part of her was on fire at the same time, the red-tongued flames running up shrouds, masts, and stays, and extending out to the yard arms. She stood in bold relief against the black background, lighting up the Roads and reflecting her lurid lights on the bosom of the now placid and hushed waters. Every now and then the flames would reach one of the loaded cannon and a shell would hiss at random through the darkness. About midnight came the grand finale. The magazines exploded, shooting up a huge column of firebrands hundreds of feet in the air, and then the burning hulk burst asunder and melted into the waters, while the calm night spread her sable mantle over Hampton Roads.

When members of Cobb's Legion were crossing the James River near Jamestown, over 30 miles up river from Hampton Roads, they noticed a bright flash down river, which was followed shortly thereafter by the sound of a tremendous explosion. Confederate soldiers in Suffolk also reported seeing and hearing the last gasp of the *Congress*. An eyewitness, Colonel Raleigh Colston noted that the frigate's death throes as "one of the grandest episodes of this splendid yet somber drama."

Five

SHOWDOWN IN HAMPTON ROADS

The *Monitor* finally entered Hampton Roads around 9 p.m. on March 8, 1862. The crew was shocked by the destruction and chaos left by the *Virginia*. "Our hearts were so very full," Dana Greene wrote, "and we vowed vengeance on the *Merrimac*." Worden, as ordered, anchored his ironclad near the U.S.S. *Roanoke* and reported to Captain John Marston, acting commander of the Union naval forces in Hampton Roads. Marston had received a telegraph from Gideon Welles instructing him to immediately send the *Monitor* up the Potomac to defend Washington against the Confederate ironclad. He recognized that the best defense for the nation's capital was in Hampton Roads. Thus, Marston ordered Worden to station the *Monitor* near the *Minnesota* and to protect that ship from the *Virginia*.

Worden found a pilot, Master Samuel Howard of the bark *Amanda*, to serve on the *Monitor*, which proceeded along the Hampton Flats to the *Minnesota*. Greene and Worden then went on board the *Minnesota* to confer with her commander, Captain Gershom Van Brunt (pictured here). Van Brunt expected to float his ship at the next high tide (2 a.m.) and required no assistance. The veteran officer had little faith in the *Monitor*'s ability to stop the Confederate ironclad and indicated that if all else failed, he would destroy his ship rather than allow it to be captured. One of the *Minnesota* crew members noted how "insignificant she looked, she was but a speck on the dark blue sea at night, almost a laughable object by day." Others were jubilant that the *Monitor* had arrived. The steam frigate's chief engineer, Thomas Rae, remembered that as he shouted down to the engine room, "the *Monitor* is alongside," the crew "gave a cheer that might have been heard in Richmond." Greene told Van Brunt that the *Monitor* would do everything it could to protect the *Minnesota*. As he returned to the *Monitor*, "the *Congress* blew up, and certainly a grander sight never was seen, but it went right to the marrow of our bones." Worden and Greene remained on the deck of the ironclad waiting for the enemy vessel's return.

When morning came, the *Minnesota* was still aground. Catesby Jones and his men had breakfast just after dawn. "We began the day with two jiggers of whiskey," one elated crewman recalled, "and a hearty breakfast." The *Virginia* got underway from its Sewell's Point mooring around 6 a.m. on March 9, accompanied by the *Patrick Henry*, *Jamestown*, and *Teaser*. Due to heavy fog, the small fleet was delayed entering Hampton Roads until nearly 8 a.m. Jones saw that the *Minnesota* was still stranded on the shoal as the *Virginia* closed within range. At 8:30 a.m., Lieutenant Charles Simms's stern Brooke rifle sent the first shot through the *Minnesota*'s rigging. The *Virginia*'s crew expected to make short work of the *Minnesota*. Ashton Ramsay recounted, "We approached her slowly, feeling our way cautiously along the edge of the channel, when suddenly, to our astonishment, a black object that looked like the historic description, 'a barrel-head afloat with cheesebox on top of it,' moved slowly out from under the *Minnesota* and boldly confronted us."

The Confederates were amazed by the sight of the Union ironclad. Lieutenant Hunter Davidson (pictured here) thought at first that "the *Minnesota*'s crew are leaving her on a raft." Lieutenant James H. Rochelle of the *Patrick Henry* noted, "such a craft as the eyes of a seaman never looked upon before—an immense shingle floating in the water, with a gigantic cheesebox rising from its center; no sails, no wheels, no smokestack, no guns. What could it be?" Jones, who had been following the *Monitor*'s construction in Northern newspapers, instantly recognized it as Ericsson's iron battery.

When Worden viewed the Confederate ironclad entering Hampton Roads, he commented to several members of the crew standing on top of the turret, "Gentlemen, that is the *Merrimac*, you had better go below." The *Monitor* headed straight for the *Virginia*. Worden knew that his ironclad was the only thing that could save the *Minnesota*. Van Brunt was doubtful that his ship could be saved by the *Monitor*. William Keeler recalled "the idea of assistance or protection being offered to the huge thing by the little pygmy at her side seemed absolutely ridiculous." The *Monitor* opened fire at 8:45 a.m. and for the next four hours, the two ironclads pounded each other mercilessly with shot and shell.

The battle was primarily fought at a range of less than 100 yards. Often the ships almost touched each other as each ironclad sought to gain an advantage. Worden hoped that by firing his heavy shot, 168-pound spherical projectiles using 15 pounds of powder from his 11-inch Dahlgrens, such pounding would loosen or break the *Virginia's* iron plates. The *Monitor's* gun crews were handicapped by the U.S. Navy powder charge requirements. Tests would later prove that Dahlgrens could handle double-charges (30 pounds), and this load would have probably

been sufficient to propel a shot through the *Virginia*'s casemate. "One shot struck directly over the outboard delivery," wrote Assistant Engineer E.A. Jack, "That was our weak spot. The shot broke the backers to the shield and sent a splinter into our engine room with about enough force to carry it halfway across the ship." Fortunately for the *Virginia*, only a few iron plates were damaged during the engagement.

The *Virginia* entered the battle with a disadvantage. She had only explosive shells, hotshot, and canister to use against wooden ships. Chief Engineer Ashton Ramsay wrote, "If we had known we were to meet her, we would have at least been supplied with solid shot for our rifled cannons." E.A. Jack echoed this problem when he wrote, "Our only hope to penetrate the *Monitor*'s shield was in the rifled cannon, but as the only projectiles we had for those were percussion shells, there was barely a chance that we might penetrate our adversary's defense by a lucky shot." Thus, Jones's strategy was first to concentrate on the *Minnesota* and, if necessary, to try to ram or board the *Monitor*.

The *Monitor*'s small size and quickness frustrated the Confederates, who tried to fire at the *Monitor*'s gun ports, but found that the turret revolved too fast. Lieutenant Eggleston complained that "we never got sight of her guns except when they were about to fire into us." Eggleston was later chided during the battle by Catesby Jones (pictured here) for not firing his gun at the Union ironclad. He replied to the *Virginia*'s commander, "It is quite a waste of ammunition to fire at her. Our powder is precious, sir, and I find I can do the *Monitor* as much damage by snapping my finger at her every five minutes."

The *Monitor*'s turret truly amazed the Confederates, yet the Federal shot continued to bounce off the sloped, iron sides of the *Virginia*. The scene aboard the *Virginia* was likened to a page from Dante's *Inferno*, as Chief Engineer Ashton Ramsay later wrote:

> On our gun deck, all was bustle, smoke, grimy figures and stern commands, while down in the engine and boiler rooms the 16 furnaces were belching out fire and smoke and the firemen standing in front of them, like so many gladiators, tugged away with devil's claw and slice-bar, inducing by their exertions more and more intense combustion and heat. The noise of the cracking, roaring fires, escaping steam, and the loud and labored pulsations of the engines, together with the roar of battle above and the thud and brations of the huge masses of iron which were hurled against us, produced a scene and sound to be compared only with the poet's picture of the lower regions.

This is a photograph of one of the *Virginia*'s many soldier-sailors, William H. Young.

Secretary of War Edwin Stanton was one of several Union leaders who thought that it was "painfully ludicrous" that the U.S. Navy would send an untried, experimental, two-gun vessel against the apparently invincible Confederate ironclad. The crew had their own concerns as well, most of which were dispelled when the *Virginia*'s first shots failed to penetrate the iron sides of the turret. The scene in the turret was similar to that on the *Virginia*, as Assistant Paymaster William Keeler later wrote:

> The sounds of the conflict were terrible. The rapid fire of our guns amid the clouds of smoke, the howling of the *Minnesota*'s shells, which were firing broadsides just over our heads (two of her shots struck us), mingled with the crash of solid shot against our sides (not from the *Virginia*) and the bursting of shells all around us. Two men had been sent down from the turret, knocked senseless by balls striking outside the turret while they happened to be in contact with the inside wall of the turret.

MELLAN DÄCK

JOHN ERICSSON

KAPTENENS KAJUTA

DET INRE AF TORNET

Despite all of its technological advantages, there were numerous problems on board the Federal ironclad. The turret did not perform precisely as designed. The port stoppers proved to be almost too heavy to operate and only one gun could be fired at a time. Lieutenant Dana Greene, in command of the turret, eventually decided to leave both ports open. Greene, who aimed each Dahlgren before it was fired, noted that his "only view of the world outside . . . was over the muzzles of the guns, which cleared the ports by only a few inches." The open ports became a necessity to enhance the gun crews' vision since the communication system between the pilothouse and turret failed to perform. Assistant Paymaster Keeler and captain's clerk Daniel

Toffey were used as runners to convey orders from Worden to Greene. "Both being landsmen," Greene later noted, "our technical communications sometimes miscarried." The men in the turret virtually lost all sense of direction due to the limited vision. White marks were painted on the stationary deck below the turret to indicate bow and stern and port and starboard. These marks, however, were obliterated early in the battle by gunsmoke residue. The men, nevertheless, struggled at the guns, "perspiration falling from them like rain," firing a round every ten minutes or so. The field of fire was limited. The guns could not fire at the Confederate ironclad when facing the bow because the pilothouse was in the way.

The *Monitor*'s turret rotating mechanism also malfunctioned. The volumes of seawater that had nearly swamped the ironclad during her stormy trip to Hampton Roads caused many iron parts to begin to rust. Consequently, the turret could not be stopped with any precision, making it virtually impossible to make well-aimed shots. Eventually, the guns were discharged "on the fly" as the turret turned past the target. Once the turret turned away from the Confederate ironclad, it was stopped to begin the loading procedure.

The two ironclads continued to circle each other, both ships striving to find a weak point in its opponent's armor. The *Monitor* had effectively blocked the *Virginia*'s path to the motionless *Minnesota*. Van Brunt noted how the Union ironclad, "much to my astonishment, laid herself right alongside of the *Merrimac*, and the contrast was that of a pygmy to a giant." After almost two hours of combat, Worden ordered the *Monitor* out of action to replenish ammunition in the turret. Cannonballs were hoisted up from a storage bin below decks through a scuttle, which required the turret to be stationary. It was a slow and laborious process, during which time Worden actually went out on deck to inspect the *Monitor* for any damage.

Catesby Jones immediately took advantage of the lull and moved the *Virginia* toward the *Minnesota*. The Confederate ironclad, leaking at its bow due to the loss of its ram from the day before, now ran aground and was unable to defend itself. The *Virginia* was in serious danger. The *Monitor* approached and, according to Ashton Ramsay, the Union ironclad:

> Began to sound every chink in our armor—everyone but that which was actually vulnerable, had she known it. The coal consumption of the two day's fight had lightened our prow until our unprotected submerged deck was almost awash. The armor on our sides below the waterline had been extended but about three feet, owing to our hasty departure before the work was finished. Lightened as we were, these exposed portions rendered us no longer an ironclad, and the *Monitor* might have pierced us between wind and water had she depressed her gun.

"Fearing that she might discover our vulnerable 'heel of Achilles,' we had to take all chances," continued Ramsay. "We lashed down the safety valves, heaped quick-burning combustibles into the already raging fires, and brought the boilers to a pressure that would have been unsafe under ordinary circumstances. The propeller churned the mud and water furiously, but the ship did not stir. We piled on oiled cotton waste, splits of wood, anything that would burn faster than coal. It seemed impossible that the boilers could stand the pressure we were crowding upon them. Just as we were beginning to despair, there was a perceptible movement, and the *Merrimack* slowly dragged herself off the shoal by main strength. We were saved."

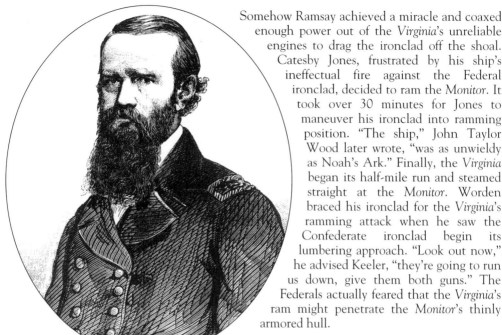

Somehow Ramsay achieved a miracle and coaxed enough power out of the *Virginia*'s unreliable engines to drag the ironclad off the shoal. Catesby Jones, frustrated by his ship's ineffectual fire against the Federal ironclad, decided to ram the *Monitor*. It took over 30 minutes for Jones to maneuver his ironclad into ramming position. "The ship," John Taylor Wood later wrote, "was as unwieldy as Noah's Ark." Finally, the *Virginia* began its half-mile run and steamed straight at the *Monitor*. Worden braced his ironclad for the *Virginia*'s ramming attack when he saw the Confederate ironclad begin its lumbering approach. "Look out now," he advised Keeler, "they're going to run us down, give them both guns." The Federals actually feared that the *Virginia*'s ram might penetrate the *Monitor*'s thinly armored hull.

The more nimble Union vessel was able to veer away right before the Confederate ironclad struck. Thus, the *Monitor* was hit only with a glancing blow. According to William Keeler, the "heavy jar nearly throwing us from our feet." The Confederates thought they had seriously damaged the *Monitor*, thinking that they had made the Union ironclad "reel beneath our terrible blow." Jones's order to reverse the engines just before striking the *Monitor* lessened the collision's impact. Since the *Virginia*'s ram, unbeknownst to Jones, was imbedded in the *Cumberland*, the ramming caused minimal damage to the *Monitor*. The only visual evidence of the ramming was that several wooden splinters from the *Virginia*'s hull left a minor indentation in the *Monitor*'s iron plate. The *Virginia* suffered damage from this tactical maneuver. The collision caused another leak in the Confederate vessel's bow. Furthermore, when the *Virginia* hit the Union ironclad, Dana Greene fired both Dahlgrens almost simultaneously at the Confederate ironclad. The shots struck the *Virginia*'s casemate just above the stern pivot gun port, forcing the shield in 2 to 3 inches and knocking down several men. "Another shot at the same place," John Taylor Wood noted, "would have penetrated."

Jones also considered the feasibility of boarding the *Monitor*. A group of volunteers was organized to leap onto the *Monitor*'s deck, cover the pilothouse with a coat to blind the ship, and toss specially prepared grenades into the turret and down the funnels. At one moment during the engagement, Worden anticipated that the Confederates might attempt to board his ship and ordered Greene to load the Dahlgrens with canister. The *Monitor* quickly slipped past the *Virginia*, and the Confederates were unable to launch such a bold and desperate attack. This is a photograph of Captain Reuben T. Thom, commander of the *Virginia*'s Marine detachment.

The *Monitor*'s evasive action during the *Virginia*'s ramming attack enabled Jones to once again maneuver toward the *Minnesota*. Several shots were sent against the stranded frigate, starting a fire on the *Minnesota*. One shell struck the tug *Dragon*. The *Dragon*'s boiler burst and the tug, which had been alongside the *Minnesota* to tow that vessel to safety, sunk.

Worden was once again able to steer his ship between the Confederate ironclad and the Union frigate. He now decided to ram the *Virginia*, seeking to strike the larger ironclad's vulnerable propeller and rudder. The *Virginia* was riding high in the water, and Worden could see the propeller churning. The *Monitor*'s captain realized that an effective strike could disable the propeller or rudder, thereby leaving the Confederate ironclad adrift and subject to capture. The *Monitor* steamed toward the *Virginia*'s fantail, but missed her target at the very last moment because of a malfunctioning steering system.

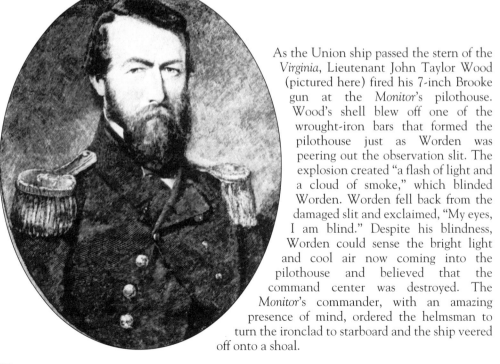

As the Union ship passed the stern of the *Virginia*, Lieutenant John Taylor Wood (pictured here) fired his 7-inch Brooke gun at the *Monitor*'s pilothouse. Wood's shell blew off one of the wrought-iron bars that formed the pilothouse just as Worden was peering out the observation slit. The explosion created "a flash of light and a cloud of smoke," which blinded Worden. Worden fell back from the damaged slit and exclaimed, "My eyes, I am blind." Despite his blindness, Worden could sense the bright light and cool air now coming into the pilothouse and believed that the command center was destroyed. The *Monitor*'s commander, with an amazing presence of mind, ordered the helmsman to turn the ironclad to starboard and the ship veered off onto a shoal.

Several officers helped Worden out of the pilothouse and sent for the ship's executive officer, Samuel Dana Greene. Greene finally made his way from the turret and found Worden, "a ghostly sight with his eyes closed and the blood apparently rushing from every pore in the upper part of his face." Greene, along with the ship's surgeon, Dr. Daniel C. Longue, escorted Worden to his cabin. Worden then told Greene that he was seriously wounded and directed the young lieutenant to take command of the ironclad. Dana Greene then asked Worden what he should do. Worden replied, "Gentleman, I leave it with you, do what you think best. I cannot see, but do not mind me. Save the *Minnesota* if you can."

The *Minnesota*'s captain immediately noticed that something was wrong with the *Monitor*. Van Brunt feared for the worse and began making preparations to scuttle his ship. Catesby Jones could also see that the *Monitor* was damaged. He believed that the "*Monitor* has given up the fight and run into shoal water." The *Virginia*'s commander decided to resume the attack against the *Minnesota*, but the pilots warned him that the tide was falling fast and the huge ironclad should move back into the Elizabeth River. Jones lamented to Ashton Ramsay that the "pilots will not place us nearer to the *Minnesota*, and we cannot run the risk of getting aground again." Jones then walked along the gundeck conferring with his officers. He quickly reviewed with each of them the circumstances of the *Monitor*'s apparent retreat and the inability of the ship's deep draught to move any closer than a mile to the *Minnesota*. He summarized the situation by stating, "this ship is leaking from the loss of her prow; the men are exhausted by being so long at their guns; . . . . I propose to return to Norfolk for repairs. What is your opinion?" A majority argued for the return to Norfolk. Jones, noting that "had there been any sign of the *Monitor*'s willingness to renew the contest we would have remained to fight her," turned the *Virginia* away from the *Minnesota* and steamed toward Sewell's Point. This is a photograph of a member of one of the *Virginia*'s gun crews, Midshipman Robert Chester Foute.

The *Virginia* fired its last shell at the *Monitor* from John Taylor Wood's stern Brooke gun at 12:10 p.m. Just as the *Virginia* steamed away, Dana Greene re-entered the *Monitor*'s pilothouse and upon seeing that the damage was minimal ordered the Union ironclad back into action. It had taken almost 30 minutes for Greene to assume command, and the lull prompted the *Virginia* to break off action. Greene mistook the *Virginia*'s course toward Sewell's Point as a sign of defeat and proclaimed, "we had evidently finished the *Merrimac*." The young lieutenant, however, did not order the *Monitor* to follow up its believed victory by attacking the *Virginia* as it left Hampton Roads. He later explained, "We had definite orders to act on the defensive, and protect the *Minnesota* . . . . Therefore, after the *Merrimack* retreated, we went to the *Minnesota* and remained by her side until she was afloat. General Wool and Secretary Fox both have complimented me very highly for acting as I did and said it was the strict military plan to follow. This is the reason we did not sink the *Merrimack*, and everyone on her says we acted exactly right." Alban Stimers immediately telegraphed John Ericsson with the message, "you have saved this place to the nation by furnishing us with the means to whip an ironclad frigate that was, until our arrival, having it all her way with our most powerful vessels!"

When Worden was told that the *Monitor* was victorious and had saved the *Minnesota*, he meekly said from his bed, "Then I can die happy." The injured officer was immediately transferred from the ironclad by Lieutenant H.A. Wise and sent on an overnight boat to Baltimore for the best available medical attention. Worden was considered the true hero of the battle and was lionized throughout the North. Eventually, he was taken to Washington to recover, and Lincoln actually visited him in sickbed at Lieutenant Wise's home. The wounded Worden said to Lincoln, "You do me great honor, Mr. President, and I am only sorry I can't see you." Lincoln replied, "You have done me more honor, sir, than I can ever do to you."

Once the battle was over, small boats flocked to the *Monitor* to congratulate the crew on their splendid victory. Assistant Secretary of the Navy Gustavus Vasa Fox, who observed the entire engagement, went on board the Union ironclad and told the *Monitor*'s officers, "Well, gentlemen, you don't look as though you just went through one of the greatest naval conflicts on record." "No, sir," Greene replied, "we haven't done much fighting, merely drilling the men at the guns a little." The exhausted Greene (pictured here) wrote home later that evening, "I had been up so long, and been under such a state of excitement, that my nervous system was completely run down . . . . My nerves and muscles twitched as though electric shocks were continually passing through them . . . . I laid down and tried to sleep—I might as well have tried to fly."

Neither ship had been seriously damaged during the four-hour battle. The Union ironclad fired 41 shots at the *Virginia* (approximately 20 of which struck the ironclad). In turn, the *Monitor* was hit 23 times by shells from the Confederate vessel. Other than Worden, who would eventually recover sight in his right eye but would be permanently disfigured, there were no serious casualties on either vessel. Nevertheless, the battle was considered by one Union soldier as "one of the greatest Naval Engagements that has ever ocurred [sic] since the Beginning of the world." The *Norfolk Day Book* reported that this "successful and terrible work will create a revolution in naval warfare, and henceforth iron will be the king of the seas." The battle received immediate international attention. The *London Times* reported, "Whereas we had available for immediate purposes one hundred and forty-nine first-class war-ships, we have now two, these two being the Warrior and her sister Ironside." Great Britain immediately committed itself to building a fleet of ironclad vessels as Lord Paget, Secretary of the Admiralty, noted in Parliament, "No more wooden ships would be built." The showdown in Hampton Roads between the *Monitor* and *Virginia* proved once and for all the power of iron over wood.

Over 20,000 soldiers, sailors, and civilians had witnessed the battle and everyone recognized the engagement as a "day of stirring events." "The next morning at 8 o'clock we got under way and stood through the fleet," Dana Greene later wrote about the *Monitor*'s victory procession in Hampton Roads. "Cheer after cheer went up from the frigates and small craft for the glorious little *Monitor* and happy, indeed, we did all feel. I was the captain of the vessel that had saved Newport News, Hampton Roads, Fortress Monroe, (as General Wool himself said) and perhaps your Northern ports." The Confederates were equally jubilant. Confederate Secretary of State Judah Benjamin sent propaganda messages to European nations stating that the "success of our iron-clad steamer *Virginia* (late the *Merrimac*) in destroying three first class frigates in her first battle, evinces our ability to break for ourselves the much-vaunted blockade, and ere the lapse of ninety days we hope to drive from our waters the whole blockading fleet." Others were not quite as confident. Catesby Jones stated that the "destruction of those wooden vessels was a matter of course especially so, being at anchor, but in not capturing that ironclad, I feel as if we had done nothing." A church service was held on the *Virginia*'s deck on March 10. Reverend J.H.D. Wingfield of Portsmouth's Trinity Church stated, "The sunshine of a favoring Providence beams upon every countenance," and declared, "the fierce weapons of our insolent invaders are broken." The inset is a photograph of one of the battle's spectators, Private Daniel O'Conner of the U.S.S. *Cumberland*'s Marine Guard.

Even though both sides claimed victory, the battle, according to Ashton Ramsay, "was a drawn one." The *Monitor* had indeed won a tactical victory, as the Union ironclad had stopped the *Virginia* from destroying the *Minnesota*, relieving Federal fears of a broken blockade and an attack on Northern cities. The battle, however, had even more immediate implications than being a major turning point in naval warfare, as the undefeated *Virginia* controlled Hampton Roads. The Confederate ironclad blocked the entrance to the James River; thereby, defending the water approach to Norfolk and Richmond. The mere existence of the *Virginia* would have a powerful influence on Major General George Brinton McClellan's strategic initiative to capture the Confederate capital in Richmond by way of the Virginia Peninsula. Brigadier General John Gross Barnard, chief engineer of the Army of the Potomac, lamented that the "*Merrimac* . . . proved so disastrous to our subsequent operations."

Six

GAVE HER TO THE FLAMES

The *Virginia*'s strategic victory closed the James River and Hampton to the Federals. Simultaneously, General McClellan decided to march toward Richmond by way of the Virginia Peninsula. McClellan's original plan entailed the use of both the James and York Rivers. Gunboats could guard his flanks, while steamers could transport supplies as McClellan's troops moved up the Peninsula. The entire concept was now in jeopardy because of the Confederate ironclad. McClellan wired Assistant Secretary of the Navy Gustavus Fox at Fort Monroe, "Can I rely on the *Monitor* to keep the *Merrimack* in check, so that I can make Fort Monroe a base of operations?" Fox replied, "The *Monitor* is more than a match for the *Merrimack*, but she might be disabled in the next encounter . . . The *Monitor* may, and I think will, destroy the *Merrimack* in the next fight; but this is hope, not certainty . . . ." McClellan held a council of war with his corps commanders and it was agreed to proceed with the campaign using only the York River. The U.S. Navy was expected to neutralize the *Virginia* and help destroy the Confederate batteries on the York River. This 1862 sketch by Alfred Waud of the C.S.S. *Teaser* shelling Union batteries on Newport News Point depicts the Confederate control of Hampton Roads.

Major General John Ellis Wool, commander of the Union Department of Virginia at Fort Monroe, concurred with Fox's opinion. He had already received orders on March 9 from McClellan to hold Fort Monroe "at all hazard" against the Confederate ironclad. Wool immediately began to block the *Virginia*'s access into the Chesapeake Bay by mounting a 15-inch Rodman Gun, nicknamed the "Lincoln Gun," next to the 12-inch "Union Gun" on the beach near the Old Point Comfort Lighthouse. The Union general was sure that the *Monitor*, supported by these two powerful guns, would effectively close the mouth of Hampton Roads to any sortie by the *Virginia*.

Regardless of Wool's preparations, the *Virginia* continued to influence the U.S. Navy's ability to support McClellan's campaign. McClellan later wrote, "The James River was declared by the naval authorities closed to the operations of their vessels by the combined influence of the enemy's batteries on its banks and the Confederate steamers *Merrimac*, *Yorktown*, *Jamestown*, and *Teaser*. Flag Officer Goldsborough . . . regarded it (and no doubt justly) as his highest and most imperative duty to watch and neutralize the *Merrimac*, and as he designed using his most powerful vessels in a contest with her, he did not feel able to attack the water batteries at Yorktown and Gloucester. All this was contrary to what had been previously stated to me and materially affected my plans. At no time during the operations against Yorktown was the Navy prepared to lend us any material assistance in its reduction until after our land batteries partially silenced the works." Welles advised McClellan that "the Confederate ship was an ugly customer." Even though the Secretary of the Navy believed the *Monitor* to be the superior vessel, Welles thought that the Union ironclad "might easily be put out of action in her next engagement and that it was unwise to place too great dependence on her." Consequently, Goldsborough (pictured here) feared that the Confederate ironclad would again strike the Union fleet. Until the other Union ironclads under construction arrived, Goldsborough was content to remain on the defensive.

The *Monitor* was recognized as the only real defense against the Confederate ironclad. William Keeler noted, "we shall remain here as guardians of Fortress Monroe and the small amount of shipping which will remain in harbour, have been ordered off in apprehension of the reappearance of the *Merrimac*. We shall remain here to meet her. We are very willing and anxious for another interview." The *Monitor*'s crew might have been ready to re-engage the *Virginia*; the Federal command was not. Gideon Welles sent a telegram on March 10 stating, "It is directed by the President that the *Monitor* be not too much exposed, and that in event shall any attempt be made to proceed with her unattended to Norfolk." Restrained by this directive, the Union ironclad also went through a change of command. While Dana Greene proved his leadership skills during the voyage to Hampton Roads and in battle with the *Virginia*, he was considered too young and inexperienced to permanently replace the wounded Worden. Lieutenant Thomas O. Selfridge, formerly of the U.S.S. *Cumberland*, relieved him of command the day after the battle. On March 12, Selfridge was replaced by Lieutenant William N. Jeffers. The 38-year-old Jeffers was an 1846 Annapolis graduate and an ordnance expert. He was not popular with the ironclad's crew, lacking, according to William Keeler, "that noble kindness of heart and quiet unassuming manner to both officers and men which endeared Captain Worden to all on board."

The *Monitor* also received some immediate alterations to prepare her for the next encounter with the *Virginia*. The pilothouse was considered one of the *Monitor*'s greatest weaknesses, and Stimers placed a shell of solid oak covered with 3 inches of wrought iron, laid in three layers, around the structure. The sides were reconfigured from perpendicular to a slope of 30 degrees to deflect shot. Worden advised from his recovery bed that the Union ironclad was susceptible to enemy boarding. Accordingly, small arms, muskets, grenades, and cutlasses were stored in the turret to help repel any boarders.

Mallory's faith in the Confederate ironclad was vindicated by the *Virginia*'s actions on March 8 and 9, 1862. The Confederate Secretary of the Navy believed that the *Virginia* had won "the most remarkable victory which naval annals record" and dreamed that the ironclad would soon steam to New York, where "she could shell and burn the city and shipping. Such an event would eclipse all the glories of the combat of the sea . . . and would strike a blow from which the enemy could never recover." The *Virginia*'s officers, however, were not as ecstatic about their ironclad's performance on March 9. John Taylor Wood advised Mallory that in "the *Monitor* we had met our equal." Buchanan wrote Mallory on March 19 in response to the secretary's letter he had received just before taking the *Virginia* into combat. "The *Virginia* is yet an experiment, and by no means invulnerable as has already been proved in her conflict on the 8 and 9," the newly promoted admiral wrote. "The *Virginia* may probably succeed in passing Old Point Comfort and the Rip Raps . . . She has then to be tested in a seaway . . . Should she encounter a gale, or a very heavy swell, I think it more than probable she would founder." In conclusion, Buchanan counseled, "the *Virginia* [is] the most important protection to the safety of Norfolk."

Since the *Virginia* was actually unfinished when it attacked the Union fleet on March 8 and had suffered significant damage during two days of combat, the ironclad was immediately placed in drydock upon its return to Gosport Navy Yard for modification and repair. John Mercer Brooke recognized that the *Virginia*'s ordnance required improved armor-piercing shot and by March 10, he was already at work producing wrought-iron, steel-tipped bolts for the 7- and 6.4-inch rifles. A new ram was also required. Brooke designed a new 12-foot-long, steel-pointed iron ram that extended the ironclad's bow 14 feet. Naval Constructor John Porter supervised repairs, often at odds with Brooke. Nevertheless, the port shutters were finally fitted onto the gunports. Battle damage to the shield necessitated the replacement of several 2-inch plates. One shipyard worker noted that "shots had plowed up the roofing so that you could lay a large watermelon in the spot where the shot had struck." Even greater attention was given to one of the *Virginia*'s primary flaws: lack of armor below the eaves of the casemate to protect the ironclad's knuckle. Time and available resources limited this effort. Eventually only a band of 2-inch plates extending 3.5 feet below the eaves and covering 160 feet on both sides was installed.

The *Virginia* also needed a new commander to replace the wounded Franklin Buchanan. Mallory appointed the 67-year-old Georgian, Flag Officer Josiah Tattnal on March 21 to assume command of all naval forces in Virginia's waters. Tattnal had joined the U.S. Navy in 1812 and fought in his first battle on Craney Island in 1813. He served with distinction in the Algerian War and Mexican War as well as in China as commander of the East India Squadron. Josiah Tattnal was known as the "beau ideal of a naval officer." Many fellow officers believed that Tattnal "possessed all the traits which are found in heroic characters." Almost 6 feet tall with long arms and a protruding lower lip, Tattnal was feared in his younger days as a cutlass expert. Tattnal resigned his U.S. Navy commission when Georgia left the Union and served as commander of the Savannah Squadron until assigned to the C.S.S. *Virginia*. His directive from Mallory was to make the Confederate ironclad "as destructive and formidable to the enemy as possible." Mallory later told Tattnal, "Do not hesitate or wait for orders, but strike when, how, and where your judgment may dictate."

"I suggest Captain Tattnal," Mallory wrote, "that you converse with Buchanan as to the power and character of the ship. The heavy iron covering designed to shield her beneath her eaves of her casement will be put on upon the first opportunity. The enemy it seems believes her to be disabled—and to be undergoing extensive repairs, and hence we may be able to surprise him, and strike him a heavy blow in the Roads." Repairs to the *Virginia*, however, were plagued by the Brooke-Porter disagreements over design modifications and lack of iron plate. Mallory fumed over the delays. Furthermore, the Confederacy had begun the construction of a second ironclad at Gosport. The C.S.S. *Richmond* was 171 feet in length with an 11-foot draft. She was to be armed with six guns, including four 7-inch Brooke rifles, and appeared specifically designed as a counter to the *Monitor*. Yard Commandant French Forrest argued that instead of building a new ironclad, the Confederacy should transform the sloop of war *Germantown*, raised following Gosport's capture, into an ironclad. Mallory disapproved. He wanted the work on the *Richmond* and *Virginia* immediately completed.

Forrest's delays did not endear him to the Confederate Secretary of the Navy. Mallory wrote, "The work of getting out the *Virginia* and the other iron-plated gunboats in course of construction at Norfolk, ready for sea, at the earliest possible moment is the most important duty, and yet this department is ignorant of any progress made upon any of the vessels, especially the *Virginia* since it went into dock. She must be prepared for sea as soon as possible." Mallory believed that Forrest had expended all of his energy preparing the *Virginia* for her first encounter with the Federal fleet and could no longer organize the repair work in a timely manner. Consequently, Captain Sidney Smith Lee, brother of General Robert E. Lee, was selected on March 24, 1862, as the new commandant of the Gosport Navy Yard. Lee (pictured here on the right) was ordered to have the *Virginia* "ready to move at any moment" and to "spare no expense" with the ironclad's refitting. Workers labored around the clock on both ironclad projects, and Lee even advertised in North Carolina for additional workmen to help finish the *Richmond*. McClellan's troops were already arriving at Fort Monroe by late March. John Bankhead Magruder wrote Tattnal, "Enemy transports are ready to pass his large army across the lower James River, or to ascend it. In either case, the consequences may be disastrous, but if he can be prevented we have the advantage. The whole depends upon the *Virginia*. From all indications on this side, the enemy may be expected to move at any moment. He will depend upon his transports whether to cross or to ascend. If they can be destroyed, he is stopped or forced to march up the peninsula; in the latter case we can concentrate and prevent him and thus save Norfolk and Richmond."

The *Virginia* left drydock on April 4, 1862. Tattnal was instructed by Mallory to attack the Union transports in Hampton Roads which, in turn, the *Virginia*'s commander hoped would provoke the *Monitor* into battle. Bad weather and mechanical problems delayed the *Virginia*'s departure for several days. As the *Virginia* waited to return to action, George McClellan launched his 121,000-man army up the Peninsula. The Army of the Potomac, however, was stopped in its tracks on April 5, 1862, by John Bankhead Magruder's Warwick-Yorktown Line. Magruder's ability to deceive the Union commander into believing the Confederates outnumbered the Federal Army prompted McClellan to besiege the Confederate defensive fortifications. Yorktown became the focus of McClellan's siege engineering. Consequently, General Robert E. Lee, then military advisor to President Jefferson Davis, wanted the *Virginia* to strike at the Union transports in the York River. Lee wrote Mallory, "I respectfully suggest for your consideration the practicability of the *Virginia*'s passing Fort Monroe in the night to the York River. She could by destroying the enemy's gunboats and transports thwart this design. After affecting this object she could again return to Hampton Roads under cover of night. I would, however, recommend that the *Virginia*, previously to an attempt against the enemy in the York River, should strike a blow at their transports and shipping in Hampton Roads and the bay outside of Forts Monroe and Calhoun, so to prevent its moving against Richmond, while she could deter any movement against Norfolk." Obviously, Lee did not understand the *Virginia*'s limitations. Mallory did, and forwarded Lee's letter to Tattnal with the admonition, "I regard the *Virginia* of the first importance to the safety of Norfolk, and hence, though the suggestion of General Lee of a dash at the enemy in York River holds out a temptation to go at him at once, it should not be made if Norfolk is to be shortly exposed to capture." Mallory added, "A wholesome fear of the *Virginia* has, I think, induced him to abandon his plan of passing his troops from Newport News and Old Point to attack Norfolk, for his present more tardy operations on the peninsula. Could you destroy his transports you would scatter his army to the winds."

Tattnal knew that his ironclad's engines were unreliable and he did not believe that the *Virginia* could pass the Union forts without serious damage. He wrote Mallory, "I have been aware from the first that my command is dangerous to my reputation, from the expectations of the public, founded on the success of Commodore Buchanan, and I have looked to a different field from his to satisfy them. I shall never find in Hampton Roads the opportunity my gallant friend found." Nevertheless, Tattnal was willing to take on the *Monitor*, declaring, "I will take her! I will take her if hell's on the other side of her!"

On April 11, at 6 a.m. Tattnal's squadron moved down the Elizabeth River to Sewell's Point. Tattnal made a brief patriotic speech to the *Virginia*'s crew and concluded, "Now you go to your battle stations, and I'll go to mine." Josiah Tattnal then perched himself in an armchair on the top deck. The *Virginia* entered Hampton Roads at 7:10 a.m., and the Federal transports scattered to the protection of Fort Monroe "like a flock of wild fowl in the act of flight." The *Monitor*, now reinforced by the iron-hulled *Naugatuck* armed with one 100-pounder Parrott rifle, stayed in the channel between Fort Monroe and the Rip Raps. The Union ironclad had strict orders not to engage the *Virginia* unless the Confederate ironclad moved out of Hampton Roads into the open waters of the Chesapeake Bay. Tattnal refused to take his ironclad out of Hampton Roads and the *Monitor* would not accept the *Virginia*'s challenge. "Each party steamed back and forth before their respective friends till dinner time," wrote William Keeler of the *Monitor*, "each waiting for the other to knock the chip out his shoulder . . . ." Keeler summarized the stand-off between the two ironclads, "She had no desire to come under fire of the Fortress and all the gunboats, to say nothing of the rams, while engaged with us, neither did the *Monitor* with her two guns desire to trust herself to the tender mercies of the gun boats and Craney island and Sewall's [sic] point batteries while trying the iron hull of the monster. I had a fine view of her at the distance of about a mile through a good glass and I tell you she is a formidable-looking thing. I had but little idea of her size and apparent strength until now."

"Had the *Merrimac* attacked the *Monitor* where she was and still is stationed by me, I would instantly have been down before the former with all my force," Goldsborough commented about the *Virginia*'s excursion. "The salvation of McClellan's army, among other things," Goldsborough continued, "greatly depends upon my holding the *Merrimac* steadily and securely in check and not allowing her to get past Fort Monroe and so before Yorktown. My game therefore is to remain firmly on the defense unless I can fight on my own terms . . . ." Goldsborough's terms, as interpreted by William Keeler, was "to get the *Merrimac* in deep water where the larger steamers fitted up as rams can have a chance at her . . . ." Tattnal understood the Union plan to "get me in close conflict with *Monitor* . . . to seize the opportunity to run into me with the *Vanderbilt* and other vessels . . . ." The 1,700-ton side-wheel *Vanderbilt* (pictured here) was donated to the U.S. Navy by multi-millionaire ship owner Cornelius Vanderbilt. The *Vanderbilt*'s bow was reinforced specifically to ram the *Virginia*.

The Confederates had concocted their own plan to destroy or capture the *Monitor*. Information gleaned from an issue of *Scientific American*, which contained a detailed report on the Union ironclad, indicated that the *Monitor* could be boarded and captured by disabling the crew. "We had four of our small gunboats," wrote Midshipman R.C. Foute, "ready to take the party, some of each division in each vessel. One division was provided with grappling irons and lines, another with wedges and mallets, another with tarpaulins, and the fourth with chloroform, hand grenades, etc. The idea was for all four vessels to pounce upon the *Monitor* at one time, wedge the turret, deluge the turret by breaking bottles of chloroform on the turret top, cover the pilot house with a tarpaulin and wait for the crew to surrender." Foute added that the "plan was very simple, and seemingly entirely practical, provided we should not be blown out of the water before it could be executed." This is a photograph of a member of one of the forlorn-hope divisions, Midshipman Daniel M. Lee. Lee was an officer assigned to the C.S.S. *Jamestown* and son of Sidney Smith Lee.

The *Virginia* steamed around in Hampton Roads from 9 a.m. to 4 p.m. hoping that the *Monitor* would dare attack. While the Confederate ironclad held the attention of the entire Federal fleet, the C.S.S. *Jamestown*, commanded by Lieutenant Joseph N. Barney, captured two brigs and an Accomac schooner off Newport News Point and towed them to Norfolk. The *Virginia*, flying the captured transport's flags upside-down under her own colors as an act of disdain, fired several shells at the *Naugatuck* and returned to Gosport Navy Yard. Tattnal was praised for his prudent, yet gallant actions on April 11. The Northern press, however, lambasted the Union response to the *Virginia*. A correspondent of the *New York Herald* wrote, "the public are justly indignant at the conduct of our navy in Hampton Roads." William Keeler expressed the frustration of the *Monitor*'s crew over the order not to engage the *Virginia* in Hampton Roads. "I believe the Department is going to build a big glass case to put us in for fear of harm coming to us."

Goldsborough was content to wait until the ironclad U.S.S. *Galena* arrived from Norfolk before making any aggressive move into Hampton Roads. The Confederates were amazed by the Federal timidity, as John Taylor Wood wrote how "frightened they must be, with all of their forts and 3 or 400 vessels in their Navy to be afraid of our vessel." Robert E. Lee, meanwhile, continued to press for the *Virginia* to "turn her attention to the harbor of Yorktown, if it is considered safe for her under cover of night to pass Fort Monroe." Mallory finally agreed to such an evening sortie in late April. Tattnal made one attempt to strike at Yorktown under cover of darkness, but was ordered back to Norfolk by Major General Benjamin Huger. There could be no attack against Yorktown until the *Richmond* was finished. Consequently, the Confederates worked day and night to complete the other ironclad, believing that the *Richmond* could handle the *Monitor* as the *Virginia* wreaked havoc amongst the Union fleet in the York River. The *Virginia* truly needed additional support. On April 18, the *Jamestown*, *Raleigh*, and *Teaser* were sent up the James River to support Magruder's right flank. Two days later, the *Patrick Henry* and *Beaufort* were assigned to Commander John Randolph Tucker's squadron stationed off the mouth of the Warwick River. This left the *Virginia* as Norfolk's only defense against an attack by the U.S. Navy.

Time was running out for the Confederate Navy in Hampton Roads. On the evening of May 3, 1862, General Joseph Eggleston Johnston (pictured here) ordered the evacuation of the Warwick-Yorktown Line. Johnston believed that "the fight for Yorktown must be one of artillery, in which we cannot win. The result is certain; the time only doubtful." Thus, faced with defending both Norfolk and Richmond, Johnston chose to defend the Confederate capital. His retreat up the Peninsula uncovered Norfolk, forcing the Confederates to make plans to abandon the port city and naval base. When he learned of the Confederate Army's retreat, Mallory immediately telegraphed Tattnal, advising him that the Confederacy looked to the *Virginia* alone to prevent the enemy from ascending the James River.

Even though the C.S.S. *Richmond* was launched on May 1, 1862, the ironclad was far from being ready for combat. That same day, Mallory visited Portsmouth and directed Commandant S. Smith Lee to begin the evacuation of Gosport Navy Yard. All of the yard's salvageable material was dismantled and removed to Richmond, Virginia, and Charlotte, North Carolina. It was a herculean effort, made desperate by Joe Johnston's retreat from the lower Peninsula. "What a terrible necessity this is," John Taylor Wood reflected in a letter to his wife. "This is war, stern, terrible war, which our sires have brought upon us." Mallory, in an effort to save as much property as feasible, ordered Commander John Randolph Tucker's squadron to assist the evacuation. On the evening of May 5, the *Patrick Henry* and *Jamestown* steamed to Norfolk. The next evening the two gunboats returned up the James River. The *Patrick Henry* towed the incomplete ironclad *Richmond* and the unfinished gunboat *Hampton*. The *Jamestown* towed a brig containing heavy guns and ordnance supplies intended for use aboard the C.S.S. *Richmond*.

Abraham Lincoln was disenchanted with McClellan's slow progress up the Peninsula as well as the U.S. Navy's apparent inability to contend with the C.S.S. *Virginia*. Thus, President Lincoln decided to go to Fort Monroe to prompt resolute action. Lincoln arrived at Old Point Comfort on board the U.S. Revenue Cutter *Miami* during the evening of May 6, 1862. He was accompanied by Brigadier General Egbert L. Viele, Secretary of the Treasury Salmon P. Chase, and Secretary of War Edwin M. Stanton (pictured here with Lincoln).

Since McClellan was already moving up the Peninsula following the bloody Battle of Williamsburg on May 5, Lincoln's focus was on Norfolk and the C.S.S. *Virginia*. A council of war was held with General Wool (pictured here), commander of the Union Department of Virginia, and Flag Officer Goldsborough. Lincoln was still disturbed by the lack of naval action. He ordered Goldsborough to put his fleet in motion against Norfolk as well as to open the James River in support of McClellan's advance against Richmond. Following a tour of the *Monitor* and *Galena*, the President directed Goldsborough to send the *Galena*, accompanied by the *Aroostook* and *Port Royal*, "up the James River at once." Goldsborough hesitated, complaining that three vessels "are too few for the work," but finally conceded to Lincoln's command.

Commander John Rodgers of the U.S.S. *Galena* assumed command of the task force and at daybreak on May 8 entered the James River. Simultaneously, Goldsborough sent another force to shell Sewell's Point. The Federals had just learned from Confederate deserters, notably the crew of the tug *J.B. White*, that the Confederates were evacuating Norfolk. The U.S.S. *Monitor* and U.S.S. *Naugatuck*, supported by several wooden warships including the U.S.S. *Susquehanna* and U.S.S. *San Jacinto*, moved past the Rip Raps and began their cannonade of the Sewell's Point battery. When Tattnal heard the shelling, he immediately steamed down the Elizabeth River from Gosport Navy Yard to contest the Union advance. As the *Virginia* neared Sewell's Point, Tattnal realized that he faced a difficult decision. He could either send his ironclad to block Rodgers's advance up the James River or he could protect the Confederate batteries defending Norfolk. Since Rodgers was by now far enough up the James River where the *Virginia* could not reach because of her tremendous draft and due to the peremptory need to protect his base, Tattnal steamed toward the *Monitor* and the other Union ships. While it appeared a second contest between the two ironclads might occur, Goldsborough ordered the Federal squadron to withdraw to its anchorage beyond Fort Monroe. Tattnal continued to steam around in Hampton Roads for the next two hours, hoping that he might induce the *Monitor* to attack but still refusing to be baited into the channel. Finally Tattnal, disgusted with the Union lack of aggression, ordered Catesby Jones to "fire a gun to windward and take the ship back to her buoy." This act of disdain and defiance was considered most appropriate by the *Virginia*'s crew as John Taylor Wood noted, "it was the most cowardly exhibition I have ever seen . . . Goldsborough and Jeffers are two cowards."

Abraham Lincoln watched the entire action from Fort Wool. Secretary of War Stanton telegraphed Washington, D.C., "President is at this moment (2 o'clock P.M.) At Fort Wool witnessing our gunboats—three of them besides the *Monitor* and *Stevens*—shelling the rebel batteries at Sewell's Point. At the same time heavy firing up the James River indicates that Rodgers and Morris are fighting the *Jamestown* and *Yorktown* . . . . The Sawyer gun at Fort Wool has silenced one battery on Sewell's Point. The James rifle mounted on Fort Wool also does good work . . . . The troops will be ready in an hour to move." The *Virginia* stopped any landing at Sewell's Point; however, Lincoln's two-prong naval assault worked. Rodgers was now up the James River, bombarding Confederate southside positions at Fort Boykin and Fort Huger, which totally isolated Norfolk.

When Lincoln recognized that Norfolk could not be captured by a naval attack, he began a personal reconnaissance of the coastline east of Willoughby's Spit, identifying the Ocean View area as perfect for an amphibious assault. Lincoln, according to one Northern correspondent, "infused new vigor in both naval and military operations here." On the afternoon of May 9, under the cover of a naval bombardment of Sewell's Point, over 6,000 troops were ferried across the Chesapeake Bay from Fort Monroe to Ocean View in canal boats. The advance force consisting of the 10th, 20th, and 99th New York, the 16th Massachusetts, elements of the 1st New York Mounted Rifles, and three batteries of light artillery was commanded by Brigadier General Max Weber. A second wave of troops was under the command of Brigadier General Joseph K.F. Mansfield.

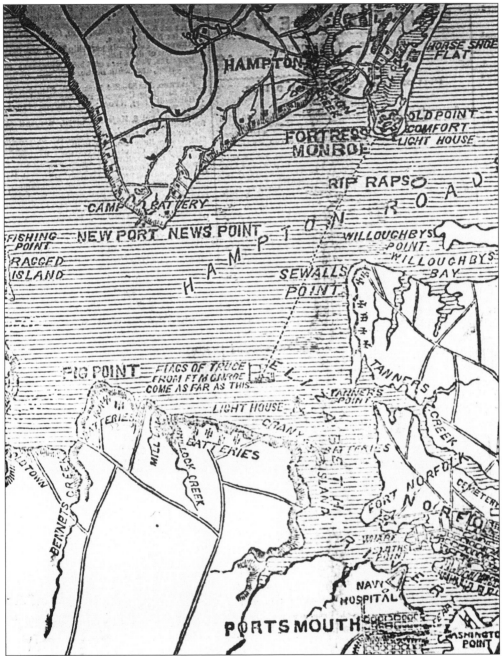

The troops were disembarked at Ocean View at dawn on May 10 without opposition. General Wool assumed command of the entire force once the Union soldiers reached Tanner's Creek. The bridge was on fire, and the Confederates fired a few artillery shells at the approaching Federals. This caused a delay; however, Wool's command reached the outskirts of Norfolk by 5 p.m., and they were met by Mayor William W. Lamb and a select committee of the municipal council of the City of Norfolk. Lamb welcomed the Union Army with a well-planned ceremony designed, according to General Viele, as "a most skillful ruse for the Confederates to secure their retreat from the city."

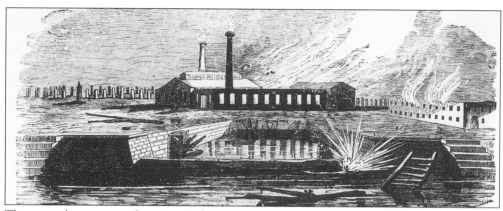

The surrender ceremony began with the "mayor, with all the formality of a mediaeval warden, appeared with a bunch of rusty keys and a formidable roll of papers, which he proceeded to read with the utmost deliberation previous to delivering the 'keys of the city.' The reading of the documents," noted General Viele, "was protracted until nearly dark. In the meanwhile the Confederates were hurrying with their artillery and stores over the ferry to Portsmouth, cutting the water-pipes and flooding the public buildings, setting fire to the navy yard, and having their own way generally, while our General was listening in the most innocent and complacent manner to the long rigmarole so ingeniously prepared by the mayor and skillfully interlarded with fulsome personal eulogium upon himself." Regardless of Viele's comments, Lamb's filibuster tactics enabled the destruction of Gosport Navy Yard and other military equipment left behind by the Confederate Army.

The Confederate Army had already evacuated Norfolk the day before the Union advance. Major General Benjamin Huger, commander of the Department of Norfolk, was seized with panic when he learned that Rodgers's squadron had moved up the James River to Jamestown Island. A 57-year-old graduate of West Point and believed to be suffering from hardening of the arteries, Huger (pictured here) feared that his 10,000-man command would be cut off from its retreat via Suffolk by the U.S. Navy. Huger left with such haste that he neglected to inform Tattnal of the evacuation.

On the morning of May 10, the *Virginia* was at her mooring off Sewell's Point when Tattnal noticed that the Confederate flag was no longer flying from the Confederate fortifications. The Sewell's Point battery appeared abandoned, so Tattnal immediately dispatched his flag lieutenant, John Pembroke Jones (pictured here), to Craney Island to find out what had happened. Jones soon learned that the Confederate Army was in retreat, the navy yard in flames, and the Union Army en route to Norfolk. Tattnal was furious. He had attended a conference with Benjamin Huger and Smith Lee on May 9, during which they decided the *Virginia* should be given ample notice of any withdrawal, enabling the Confederate ironclad to move up the James River to serve as a floating battery defending Richmond.

Tattnal was now faced with a difficult decision. He could take his ironclad out and attack the Union fleet, perhaps destroying several enemy vessels before sinking in a blaze of glory. Neither this course of action nor any effort to take the *Virginia* out to sea en route to another Southern port was advisable. Tattnal realized instead that an effort must be made to get the *Virginia* up the James River toward Richmond. The pilots advised that this could be achieved only if the huge ironclad could reduce her draft from 22 feet to 18 feet so that she could cross Harrison's Bar. The crew immediately went to work throwing coal, ballast, and everything else overboard except the ironclad's guns and ammunition. The *Virginia* had been lightened to 20 feet, but around 1 a.m. on May 11, the pilots informed Catesby Jones that the *Virginia* could not get across. The wind was from the west rather than the east, blowing the water away from the bar and making it even more shallow. Tattnal cried treason, but there was little he could do. The lightening had made the *Virginia*, according to Ashton Ramsay, "no longer an ironclad," therefore unable to engage the Federal fleet.

The *Virginia* would have to be destroyed to prevent her capture. The ironclad was run aground off Craney Island and the crew slowly debarked using the ironclad's two cutters. After three hours, the crew was safely ashore and combustibles were spread throughout the ship. Catesby Jones and John Taylor Wood set the match and then rowed for shore "by the light of our burning ship." "Still unconquered, we hauled down our drooping colors, their laurels all fresh and green," lamented Ashton Ramsay, "and with mingled pride and grief gave her to the flames." The crew then marched 20 miles to Suffolk, where Tattnal sadly telegraphed Mallory, "The *Virginia* no longer exists."

When Mallory learned of the *Virginia*'s destruction, he exclaimed, "May God protect us and cure us of weakness and folly." John Mercer Brooke blamed the *Virginia*'s destruction on "poor leadership and lack of harmony within the Government." The Federals were overjoyed, as S.R. Franklin remembered:

> It was a beautiful sight to us in more senses than one. She had been a thorn in our side for a long time, and we were glad to have her well out of the way. I remained on deck for the rest of the night watching her burning. Gradually the casemate grew hotter and hotter, until finally it became red hot, so that we could distinctly mark its outlines, and remained in this condition for fully half an hour, when, with a tremendous explosion, the *Merrimac* went into the air and was seen no more.

Seven

WRONG WAY TO RICHMOND

Norfolk's capture and the subsequent destruction of the C.S.S. *Virginia* placed Richmond in a panic. There was nothing to stop the Federal fleet from steaming straight to Richmond. Pressed by Lincoln, McClellan, and Secretary of the Navy Gideon Welles to move against the Confederate capital, Goldsborough ordered Commander John Rodgers to "push on up to Richmond, if possible, without any unnecessary delay, and shell the place into a surrender . . . . Should Richmond fall into our possession, inform me of the fact at the earliest possible moment."

The Confederates had fortified several sites on the lower James River in 1861. Fort Boykin, Fort Huger, Mulberry Island Point, Jamestown Island, and Fort Powhatan were earthen works designed to defend this approach to Richmond. Some of these forts, such as the seven-pointed star-shaped Fort Boykin, were colonial-era fortifications rebuilt to mount modern naval ordnance. Fort Boykin was shelled by Union vessels on May 8, 1862, when Rodgers's squadron first entered the James River. It was evacuated. However, Rodgers's command shelled Fort Huger on May 8 and again on May 12. Other Confederate batteries were simply abandoned and their guns spiked as Johnston's army withdrew up the Peninsula. Rodgers stopped at each fort. Consequently, his progress up river was slow.

Rodgers's squadron consisted initially of his own ship, the six-gun ironclad U.S.S. *Galena*, the 90-day gunboat U.S.S. *Aroostook*, commanded by Lieutenant John C. Beaumont, and the side wheel double-ender U.S.S. *Port Royal*. The *Port Royal* was captained by Lieutenant George Upham Morris, who had survived the sinking of the *Cumberland* on March 8, 1862. On May 12, Rodgers's command was reinforced by the U.S.S. *Monitor* and the U.S.S. *Naugatuck*. The *Naugatuck* was also called the *Stevens Battery* in honor of its builder E.A. Stevens, who had donated the one-gun, iron-hulled vessel to the U.S. Navy. The squadron reached Harrison's Landing on May 14, 1862.

The Confederate capital was in an uproar over the approach of the Union fleet. Preparations were begun by the Confederate administration to abandon Richmond, and the city's government vowed to burn the city rather than see it fall to the Union. Richmond's lack of river defenses had been an issue for several months. Robert E. Lee, however, was determined that Richmond "shall not be given up" and ordered his son, Colonel George Washington Custis Lee, to help coordinate efforts to fortify Drewry's Bluff. Custis Lee feverishly worked with local landowner and commander of the Southside Heavy Artillery, Captain Augustus H. Drewry and Commander Ebenezer Farrand of the C.S. Navy, to build gun emplacements. Drewry's Bluff was a natural defensive position on the south side of the James River. The bluff, rising over 100 feet above the river, commanded a sharp bend in the James River and was the last place available to effectively mount a defense before reaching Richmond.

A redoubt, called Fort Darling, had been constructed atop the bluff and armed with three cannon: two 8-inch Columbiads and one 10-inch Columbiad. This battery was manned by the Southside Heavy Artillery and the Bedford Artillery. Lieutenant Catesby ap Roger Jones had also been ordered to proceed to Drewry's Bluff with the *Virginia*'s officers and crew following the ironclad's destruction. Jones realized that "the enemy is in the river, and extraordinary exertions must be made to repel him," and put his men to work building additional gun emplacements. By the morning of May 15, the sailors had mounted five guns, three 32-pounders, and two 64-pounders taken from the C.S.S. *Patrick Henry* and C.S.S. *Jamestown* in a battery situated west of Captain Drewry's position. A 7-inch rifle from the *Patrick Henry* was also mounted in an earth-covered, log casemate located near the entrance to Fort Darling.

The *Jamestown* was sunk along with several other stone-laden vessels approximately 300 yards in front of Drewry's Bluff to form an obstruction. Commander John Randolph Tucker held the remaining gunboats of the James River Squadron: *Patrick Henry*, *Raleigh*, *Teaser*, and *Beaufort*. They were ready to engage any Union vessel that might make its way past the defenses. A Confederate marine detachment, commanded by Captain John D. Simms, dug rifle pits below the bluff, and Lieutenant John Taylor Wood deployed sharpshooters on the opposite bank of the river to harass the Union ships as they neared the Confederate batteries on the bluff.

Around 6:30 a.m. on May 15, Rodgers's flotilla got underway from its anchorage near the mouth of Kingsland Creek, 2 miles below Drewry's Bluff. Rodgers decided that the *Galena*'s thin armor should be tested under fire. "I was convinced as soon as I came on board that she would be riddled with shot," Rodgers later wrote, "but the public thought differently, and I resolved to give the matter a fair trial." The ironclad was constructed by Cornelius Bushnell with an experimental hull design utilizing overlapping 4-inch armor strips in the form of clapboards. The *Galena*'s sides curved from the waterline to the top deck to give the ironclad protection against shell fire from opposing ships. However, this armor-clading design would prove inadequate protection against plunging fire from Drewry's Bluff. Nevertheless, Rodgers placed the *Galena* in the lead, and by 7:45 a.m., his squadron neared the obstructions. The *Galena* steamed to within 600 yards of Drewry's Bluff and then anchored. The river was very narrow at this point, but Rodgers swung the ironclad's broadside toward the Confederate batteries. Confederate Charles H. Hasker was amazed by how Rodgers placed the *Galena* into action with such "neatness and precision." Hasker called the maneuver as "one of the most masterly pieces of seamanship of the whole war." The *Galena* received two hits while completing the maneuver and quickly became the primary target of the Confederate batteries. Once in position, however, Rodgers ordered his ironclad's port broadside battery consisting of two 9-inch Dahlgrens and one 100-pounder Parrott to open fire on the Confederate works atop the bluff.

The Federal fleet was at a distinct disadvantage. The obstructions effectively blocked any opportunity to run past the batteries toward Richmond. Rifle fire from along the river bank peppered the crews of the *Port Royal*, *Naugatuck*, and *Aroostook*. These vessels anchored about a half mile down river from the obstructions and faced their bows toward the Confederate batteries. The gunboats then shelled the bluff with their 100-pounder Parrott pivot rifles. While this deployment presented more difficult targets for the Confederate artillerists atop Drewry's Bluff, Lieutenant Morris of the *Port Royal* was forced to train his 24-pounder howitzers on the nearby shoreline to disrupt the accurate fire of Confederate sharpshooters in the woods. The *Galena* anchored "within point-blank range" of the Confederate batteries and soon the cannonade began to take effect. Ebenezer Farrand noted, "nearly every one of our shots telling upon her iron surface." Seeing that the Confederates were concentrating their fire on the *Galena*, Lieutenant Jeffers moved the *Monitor* at 9 a.m., virtually abreast of the *Galena*, in an effort to draw some of the Confederate shot away from the larger ironclad. The *Monitor*'s turret, however, did not permit the ironclad to elevate its two 11-inch Dahlgrens sufficiently to hit the Confederate batteries. Eventually, the *Monitor* backed down stream and continued a deliberate fire from its final position below the *Galena*.

Even though the plunging Confederate shot was beginning to take its toll on the *Galena*, the Confederates encountered several problems. The 10-inch Columbiad, loaded with a double charge of powder, recoiled off its platform when the first shot was fired. This heavy naval gun was not brought back into action until near the end of the engagement. The recent heavy rains caused the casemate protecting the 7-inch Brooke gun to collapse. Union shot caused 13 casualties, including several soldiers killed by fragments from a 100-pound shell fired by the *Galena*. The Confederate fire often slackened during the engagement due to a limited amount of ammunition. In addition, the Confederates often retreated into bombproofs during periods of heavy Union shelling to avoid casualties. Nevertheless, the "batteries on the Rebel side were beautifully served," noted John Rodgers of the *Galena*, "and put shot through our sides with great precision."

By 11:30 a.m., Rodgers's squadron, running low on ammunition and having braved Confederate fire for almost four hours, broke off the action and retreated down the river. The *Galena* suffered the greatest damage. The fight demonstrated that the ironclad was "not shot proof." William Keeler of the *Monitor* commented that the *Galena*'s "iron sides were pierced through and through by the heavy shot, apparently offering no more resistance than an egg shell, verifying Rodgers's opinion that 'she was beneath naval criticism.' " The *Galena* was hit 43 times and 13 shots had penetrated the iron. Her railings were shot away, the smokestack riddled, and she suffered 24 casualties. When Keeler went aboard the *Galena*, he thought that the ship "looked like a slaughter house." "The sides and ceiling overhead," he later wrote, "the ropes and guns were spattered with blood and brains and lumps of flesh, while the decks were covered with large pools of half coagulated blood and strewn with portions of skulls, fragments of shells, arms, legs, hands, pieces of flesh and iron, splinters of wood and broken weapons were mixed in one confused, horrible mass." The other Union vessels also suffered some damage: the *Port Royal* received two hits below the waterline and the *Naugatuck*'s 100-pounder Parrott had burst. The *Monitor* received only three hits, none of which caused any damage.

Rodgers's squadron endured "a perfect tempest of iron raining down upon and around us . . ." until the crippled *Galena* was forced to retreat. When the Confederates saw the smoke rise from the *Galena* after a shell crashed through the ironclad's bow, the gunners on the bluff "gave her three hearty cheers as she slipped her cables and moved down the river." Lieutenant John Taylor Wood (seen here) hailed the *Monitor*'s pilothouse from the river bank, shouting, "Tell Captain Jeffers that is not the way to Richmond." The battle was a major Confederate victory and saved Richmond from capture by the U.S. Navy. Great credit was given to the crewmen of the *Virginia*, who served several cannons during the engagement. Drewry's Bluff was their last opportunity to fight the *Monitor*. The Union would not advance this far up the James River again until 1865.

Eight
CAPE HATTERAS

The U.S.S. *Monitor* remained in the James River Squadron throughout McClellan's Peninsula Campaign and then returned to Hampton Roads. Even though the ironclad needed repairs, Flag Officer Goldsborough feared that the C.S.S. *Richmond*, often called the *Merrimack II* by the Federals, would soon attack Hampton Roads. William Keeler was sick of hearing about these rumors. "Some of us will die off one of these days with *Merrimac*-on-the-brain." Keeler added that the "disease is raging furiously." William Keeler is standing in the back row, second from right, in this July 1862 photograph.

It was a monotonous and hot summer for the *Monitor*'s crew. Often temperatures inside the ironclad reached over 140 degrees, and the men below "suffered terribly for the want of fresh air." The humidity often became so oppressive at night that many braved the flies and mosquitoes to sleep on the deck.

The unpopular captain, Lieutenant William N. Jeffers, only made matters worse. Smarting from the *Monitor*'s inglorious role in the Drewry's Bluff engagement, Jeffers prepared a report criticizing the ironclad. Jeffers complained about virtually every aspect of the *Monitor*'s design and fighting qualities. He noted that the *Monitor*'s engagement with the *Virginia* "caused an exaggerated confidence to be entertained by the public in the powers of the *Monitor*" and concluded "for general purposes wooden ships . . . have not yet been superseded." Ericsson personally responded to the report, providing a detailed reply. He explained how the ironclad should work; thereby, disabusing most of Jeffers's comments. Ericsson noted that the placement of the pilothouse atop the turret was Jeffers only valid criticism. The modification during construction, however, would have caused a month long delay, and Ericsson concluded that the "damage to the national course which might have resulted from that delay is beyond computation."

Jeffers, much to the relief of the *Monitor*'s crew, was relieved of his command on August 9, 1862. He was temporarily replaced with Commander Thomas Stevens. On September 11, Commander John Pyne Bankhead (pictured here), a 41-year-old South Carolinian and cousin to Confederate general John Bankhead Magruder, was assigned as the ironclad's captain. Bankhead received orders on September 30, 1862, to take the ironclad to the Washington Navy Yard for repairs. The ship's bottom was scraped, davits and cranes were added to mount cutters, telescoping funnels were installed, and iron patches covered shell damage from the *Monitor*'s two engagements. While in the Navy Yard, the *Monitor* became Washington's premier tourist attraction. The ironclad was visited daily by all manner of curiosity seekers, who often left with various souvenirs. "When we came up to clean that night," Louis Stodder remembered, "there was not a key, doorknob, escutcheon—there wasn't a thing that hadn't been carried away."

In November, Commander Bankhead took the *Monitor* back to Hampton Roads. The *Monitor* remained at anchor off Newport News Point until Christmas Day, when orders were received to proceed to Beaufort, North Carolina. The ironclad was to assist in the blockade of Wilmington, North Carolina, on the Cape Fear River. Several of the men who had served with the *Monitor* since her commissioning remembered the harrowing voyage from New York City to Hampton Roads in March and were uncomfortable with the prospect of a similar trip. "I do not consider this steamer," Dana Greene warned, "a seagoing vessel."

The powerful 236-foot-long side-wheeler U.S.S. *Rhode Island*, which had recently arrived in Hampton Roads following a refitting in Boston's Charlestown Navy Yard, was detailed to tow the *Monitor* to Beaufort. The *Rhode Island* (pictured here) was captained by Commander Stephen Decauter Trenchard. Trenchard's ship had run aground entering the Chesapeake Bay on December 19, but was declared undamaged. The *Rhode Island* and *Monitor* were to be accompanied on their voyage south by the *State of Georgia* towing the improved monitor, U.S.S. *Passaic*.

The convoy was delayed by bad weather until December 29, 1862. The day was "clear and pleasant, and every prospect of its continuation," prompting Commander Trenchard to prepare the *Rhode Island* for its voyage. At 2:30 p.m., the *Rhode Island* took up to two towlines, attaching her to the *Monitor,* and steamed past the Virginia Capes south to North Carolina. The first evening passed without event; however, on the afternoon of December 30, the wind increased and the sea turned turbulent. By nightfall, waves began to crash over the pilothouse and water started to fill the ironclad. Bankhead informed the *Rhode Island* that if the *Monitor* needed help during the evening a red lantern would be displayed next to the ironclad's white running light.

Around 8 p.m., the *Monitor* was suddenly hit by a series of fierce squalls. The ironclad was now in "very heavy weather, riding one huge wave, plunging through the next, as if shooting straight for the bottom of the ocean." The vessel's helmsman, Francis Butts, continued his description of the effects of the heavy gale on the *Monitor* stating that the ironclad would drop into a wave "with such force that her hull would tremble, and with a shock that would sometimes take us off our feet." Water soon began to seep into the engine room from leaks caused by the pounding sea. Bankhead ordered his crew to start the Worthington Steam Pump to keep the water down. When this system proved unable to stem the rising water, the large Adams centrifugal steam pump, capable of removing 3,000 gallons a minute, was started. Since this pump also proved inadequate to stop the flow of water, which had by 9 p.m. risen over a foot deep in the engine room, Bankhead put the crew to work on the hand pumps and organized a bucket brigade. The bailing served little purpose other than to lessen the panic amongst the crew. "But our brave little craft struggled long and well," wrote William Keeler. "Now her bow would rise on a huge billow and before she could sink into the intervening hollow, the succeeding wave would strike her under her heavy armor with a report like thunder and violence that threatened to tear apart her thin sheet iron bottom and the heavy armor which it supported."

The situation had become desperate aboard the ironclad. Nothing seemed to arrest the influx of water. By 11 p.m., the furnace fires were extinguished by the ever rising seawater, rendering the *Monitor* virtually helpless. The foundering ironclad appeared "isolated in a sea of hissing, seething foam." Bankhead ordered the red lantern displayed and tried to signal the *Rhode Island* for assistance. He ordered the lines linking the two ships cut and dropped anchor to stop the ironclad's pitching. Signal flares were launched, yet the *Rhode Island* still did not notice the *Monitor*'s dilemma. "Send your boats immediately, we are sinking," Bankhead shouted at the *Rhode Island*. "Words cannot depict the agony of those moments as our little company gathered on top of the turret, stood with a mass of sinking iron beneath them, gazing through the dim light, over the raging waters and an anxiety amounting almost to agony for some evidence of succor from the only source to which we could look for relief," Keeler painfully remembered. Butts recalled, the "clouds now began to separate, a moon of about half-size beamed out upon the sea, and the *Rhode Island*, now a mile away, became visible. Signals were exchanged, and I felt that the *Monitor* would be saved . . . ."

As the *Rhode Island* backed toward the *Monitor*, one of the towlines fouled the port paddle wheel. This caused the side-wheeler to temporarily lose control and she almost collided with the sinking ironclad. The *Rhode Island*'s crew worked frantically to stabilize the steamer and launched lifeboats to retrieve the *Monitor*'s crew. It was a difficult task, and several of the *Monitor*'s crew were carried overboard as they tried to enter the lifeboats. Several men refused to make the attempt, foolishly deciding to take their chances by remaining on the ironclad. Another, Engineer G.H. Lewis, was just too ill to leave his sickbed. A total of four officers and 12 men were lost when the *Monitor* sank in 220 feet of water 15 miles south of Cape Hatteras, North Carolina. The inset is of Seaman John Jones of the *Rhode Island*, who was awarded the Congressional Medal of Honor for heroism in rescuing the *Monitor*'s crew.

"It was half past twelve, the night of the 31st of December, 1862," recalled Seaman Butts, "when I stood on the forecastle of the *Rhode Island*, watching the red and white lights that hung from the pennant staff above the turret, and which now and then were seen as we would perhaps both rise on the sea together, until at last, just as the moon had passed below the horizon, they were lost, and the *Monitor* . . . was seen no more."

Nine

IRON AGAINST WOOD

The Battle of the Ironclads is an 18-month saga highlighted by two days of fierce combat. The events on March 8 and 9, 1862, comprise the greatest naval engagement of the Civil War and, perchance, one of history's most influential sea battles. The *Virginia*'s victory on March 8, 1862, proved once and for all the superiority of armored steam-powered warships over wooden sailing vessels. It was a stunning achievement for the fledgling Confederate Navy; however, on the next day the U.S.S. *Monitor* reinforced the new power of ironclads. The *Monitor* combined a series of new technologies, highlighted by her low profile and revolving turret, and was the progenitor of the modern warship. It is not surprising, then, when the *London Times* noted that "there is not now a ship in the English navy apart from these two [H.M.S. *Warrior* and H.M.S. *Ironsides*] that it would not be madness to trust to an engagement with that little *Monitor*."

The March 9 battle proved that only an ironclad could stop another ironclad. The world's navies took immediate notice and each major power began expensive fleet rebuilding efforts. The Confederacy and Union alike recognized the strengths (and in some cases the weaknesses) of their prototypes and initiated major shipbuilding programs. The *Merrimack-Virginia* design created by the unhappy team of John Porter and John Mercer Brooke became the basic model for all other Confederate ironclads. Several huge ironclads, such as the *Louisiana* and the *Arkansas*, were built as offensive weapons to challenge the blockade. The Confederates, however, quickly realized their technological and industrial limitations. Porter modified the design into a smaller, lighter draft vessel produced for harbor defense. The first of these new style ironclads was the C.S.S. *Richmond*. This flat-bottomed and shallow-draft ironclad design would be recreated in several lengths throughout the South. The Confederacy would attempt to build over 50 ironclads; however, only 22 were commissioned. All of the Confederate ironclads were plagued by similar problems: poor propulsion systems, construction delays, limited industries producing iron and machinery, an overtaxed transportation network, and a lack of sufficient skilled workers. These factors all contrived to weaken the development of Confederate ironclads. Even so, the Southern ironclads were generally well armed with rifled Brooke guns and either fitted with a ram or a spar torpedo. Nevertheless, the Confederate ironclads did tremendous service for the Southern cause. The C.S.S. *Albemarle* tipped the balance in eastern North Carolina for several months until she was destroyed by a torpedo. Ironclads in Richmond, Charleston, and Savannah successfully defended these major port cities against Union naval attack until each city fell to Federal land-based forces. The simple casemate design proved to be the best solution for the industrially weak Confederacy.

The U.S.S. *Monitor*'s tactical victory on March 9, 1862, in Hampton Roads produced an intense appreciation in the North for Ericsson's design. Less than three weeks after the battle, Ericsson and his partners received a contract to build "6 boats on the plan of the *Monitor* for $400,000 each—they are to be trifle larger in size—this will do." Contracts were also issued to other builders to produce the *Passaic* class of monitors. Many other types of monitor-styled vessels were produced throughout the war, including double-turreted monitors such as the U.S.S. *Kickapoo* and U.S.S. *Onondaga*. Even oceangoing monitors, the *Miantonomah* class, were built during the war. The monitor design was continually modified by other shipbuilders. James Eads and Alban Stimers both created variations of low-freeboard, turreted armored warships. Even the U.S.S. *Roanoke*, originally a sister ship of the U.S.S. *Merrimack*, was converted into an ironclad. The hull was plated and three turrets were installed on the deck. While assigned to the North Atlantic Blockading Squadron, the U.S.S. *Roanoke* was not a success and spent most of the war defending New York Harbor.

The U.S.S. *Monitor* may have spawned a new era in shipbuilding, yet there were numerous flaws in the design. Monitors were basically floating batteries, having to be towed from port to port. The ships were so unseaworthy that they could not serve their primary function as blockading ships and proved to be better suited for service along inland waterways. These ironclads had insufficient armament (two guns per turret) and a slow volume of fire. Despite these problems, the *Monitor* created a revolution in warship design. The revolving, armored turret, with its concentration of guns able to fire in any direction, would dominate naval shipbuilding for the next 75 years. Warships would feature iron construction, low profile, speed, and maneuverability. The *Monitor* and *Virginia* defined the modern warship on March 9, 1862, in Hampton Roads.

The officers and crews of the two ironclads realized immediately after the battle that they were all part of something great. Perhaps only a handful recognized the battle as the dawn of modern naval warfare, yet all were lauded throughout the rest of their lives as heroes of the greatest naval engagement of the Civil War.

The two ironclads never fought each other again after March 9, 1862, nor did either of the ships survive 1862. Nevertheless, the *Monitor* and *Virginia* left in their wake a powerful legacy of ship design and heroism, which still guides naval operations today. The relics of these famous ships, such as the *Virginia*'s anchor pictured here, are powerful reminders of the showdown in Hampton Roads that forever changed naval warfare.

Photo Credits

The following images are noted by page number with "a" for first image and "b" for second image.

Casemate Museum: 8, 9, 16b, 34a, 87b, 88b, 94b, 96a, 108; Chrysler Museum of Art: 64a, 99b, 112a; City of Hampton: 79a, 83a, 111a, 112b, 127a; *Confederate State Navy*: 11a, 71a; Library of Congress: 31b, 37, 100, 101b, 118a; Library of Virginia: 6a, 14a, 15a, 16a, 18a, 21a, 23, 24,a, 25b, 26a, 34b, 64b, 65a, 72a, 84–85, 93b, 105a, 106a, 114a, 127b; Kirn Memorial Library: 36a, 53; Mariners' Museum: front cover, 4, 20, 25a, 28a, 30, 33, 38a, 41, 46, 49, 52b, 54, 55, 57b, 67, 69a, 70, 75, 93a, 97, 104b, 121, 125; Museum of the Confederacy: 26b, 35b, 38b, 66a, 68b, 72b, 73, 99a, 105b, 110b; Museum of Fine Arts, Boston, Karolik Collection: 68a; National Archives: 10, 13, 17, 24b, 78a; David Neff, Tidewater Community College: 118b; Nimitz Library, U.S. Naval Academy: 91a, 106b; Charles V. Peery: 2, 91b, 104a; John Ridgely Porter III: 27; Portsmouth Naval Shipyard Museum: 35a, 42a, 44–45, 48a, 59a; John Moran Quarstein: 14b, 15b, 18b, 31a, 36b, 79b, 86, 90a, 110a, 113, 122, 123, 124a; David Sullivan Collection: 60a, 94a; U.S. Army Military History Institute: 32b, 40a, 50, 51, 56a, 76a, 92b, 96b, 98a, 111b, 115, 116, 117, 119, 120a; U.S. Naval Historical Center: 12, 28b, 42b, 43, 47a, 48b, 52a, 58a, 61b, 66b, 82b, 89a, 103, 107b, 124 (inset); Virginia War Museum: 6b, 11b, 21b, 22, 29, 32a, 39, 40b, 47b, 56b, 57a, 58b, 59b, 61a, 62–63, 65b, 69b, 71b, 74, 76b, 77, 78b, 80–81, 82a, 83b, 87a, 88a, 89b, 90b, 92a, 95, 98b, 101a, 102, 107a, 109, 114b, 120b, 124b, 126; Jerry Wright: 19.

Acknowledgments

I am indebted to many individuals whose efforts made this comprehensive collection of images documenting the famous first battle between ironclads available for publication. The story of the *Monitor* and *Virginia* (*Merrimack*) has enthralled me since I was a young lad, so my initial expression of appreciation must be given to my parents, Mary and Vernon Quarstein, who fostered my interest in Civil War history. As with previous projects, I must thank my wonderful wife, Martha, for typing my text and supporting my work on this project. Lee Hall Mansion staff members J. Michael Moore and Sarah Goldberger collected images from various public institutions and prepared the collection for publication. Tim Smith, a Virginia War Museum board member, collected photographs from private sources and donated his considerable photographic talents to this project.

The following individuals provided unique imagery from public institutions: John Pemberton, the Mariners' Museum; Audrey C. Johnson, the Library of Virginia; David Johnson, the Casemate Museum; John Coski and Terry Hudgins, the Museum of the Confederacy; Karen Otis, Museum of Fine Arts, Boston; Linda M. Cagney, Chrysler Museum of Art; Michael Cobb, City of Hampton; Curt Sanders, Northeastern Photographics; and Alice Hanes, Portsmouth Naval Shipyard Museum. I also must thank the following collectors for providing research information, documents, and rare photographs from their personal collections: Charles V. Peery, Jerry Wright, John Ridgely Porter III, Alan Flanders, David Sullivan, David Neff of Tidewater Community College, and my son, John Moran Quarstein.